THE
FEEL-
GOOD
DIET

**The Weight-Loss Plan That
Boosts Serotonin, Improves Your Mood,
and Keeps the Pounds Off for Good**

CHERYLE HART, M.D., AND MARY KAY GROSSMAN, RD

New York Chicago San Francisco Lisbon London Madrid Mexico City
Milan New Delhi San Juan Seoul Singapore Sydney Toronto

The *McGraw-Hill* Companies

Library of Congress Cataloging-in-Publication Data

Hart, Cheryle R.
    The feel-good diet : the weight-loss plan that boosts serotonin, improves your
mood, and keeps the pounds off for good / by Cheryle R. Hart and Mary Kay Grossman.
        p.   cm.
    Includes bibliographical references and index.
    ISBN 0-07-145378-4
    1. Weight loss.   2. Reducing diets.   3. Serotonin—Receptors.   I. Grossman,
Mary Kay.   II. Title.

RM222.2.H255   2007
613.2′5—dc22   2006022553

1 2 3 4 5 6 7 8 9 10 11 12 13 14 15   DOC/DOC 0 9 8 7 6

ISBN-13: 978-0-07-145378-3
ISBN-10:   0-07-145378-4

Interior design by Think Design

McGraw-Hill books are available at special quantity discounts to use as premiums and
sales promotions, or for use in corporate training programs. For more information, please
write to the Director of Special Sales, Professional Publishing, McGraw-Hill, Two Penn
Plaza, New York, NY 10121-2298. Or contact your local bookstore.

The purpose of this book is to provide information only. It is not intended to be and
should not be relied upon as medical advice. The information in the book is not intended
to diagnose, treat, or cure any illness or medical condition. While the authors believe that
the information in the book, including the Feel-Good Diet program, is based on sound
medical research, some of the information may not apply to you. The use of alternative
treatment methods and dietary supplements are not a substitute for medications
prescribed by your doctor. If you are under a physician's care, do not make any changes in
your therapy without first consulting him or her. As with any diet program, before starting
this program you should consult your physician about your specific condition and needs.

This book is printed on acid-free paper.

Contents

Preface

Since starting the Wellness Workshop in Spokane, Washington, ten years ago, I have worked with thousands of women and men in achieving weight-loss success. In 1999, I wrote *The Insulin-Resistance Diet* to help many more people realize that their weight problem was due to their body's reaction to insulin. Managing insulin resistance is critical for controlling health issues such as weight, cholesterol, blood pressure, and diabetes. I also found that at the same time I needed to support an important brain hormone, serotonin, so that the people could maintain their weight loss. As a medical weight-loss physician, my mission is to help improve the health of my clients by providing the most up-to-date scientifically based diet and exercise methods available. In this book I have taken the latest research on serotonin and developed a new program that combines managing insulin with supporting serotonin.

Because I am the only weight-loss physician in the area, desperate dieters come to my clinic having "tried everything." My clients have been on every diet from Jenny Craig to Weight Watchers and one or two of the low-carbohydrate diets to boot. These women (most of my clients are female) are fabulous dieters. They know "points" and calories and can recite grams of fat by heart. On each diet they lost lots of weight, usually from forty to eighty pounds. But within a few months they started gaining back the weight and soon weighed even more. After a while they tried another of the latest diets, lost weight, and gained it back, plus more. This up-and-down-and-up-and-down weight cycle is so common among dieters it has been named "yo-yo dieting." After seeing this pattern for several years, I set out to determine what causes yo-yo dieting and how we can prevent it.

Another problem with yo-yo dieting is that each time you diet it gets harder and harder to lose weight. I noticed that some women even cut their food intake almost to the point of starvation and still only marginally lost weight. I have found that yo-yo dieting is very stressful on the hormones that control metabolism. Still overweight, their hormones think that they are actually starving. Could it be that their metabolism has been affected to the point where it is no longer working properly? More important, can it be recovered?

Several years ago, I started noticing another unexpected problem occurring among many of my new clients, again mostly women. They were coming to our clinic having been placed on antidepressants by their physicians during or shortly after their last diet. These women had good weight-loss success and had no previous history of depression.

They told me that the longer they dieted the more anxious, depressed, and irritable they felt. As a doctor, I did not expect to see these concerns because diets are supposed to help you feel better, not worse.

I found that most of these women had recently been on one of the popular low-carbohydrate diets, mainly Atkins or, lately, the South Beach Diet. It was while on those diets that their energy, mood, and sex drive started deteriorating. Some women became obsessed with food, thinking about it all the time. Their cravings for carbohydrates were worse than when they started on their low-carbohydrate diet. Many completely lost interest in sex. One husband admitted he would rather have his wife be at the weight she was before dieting than be "thin, bitchy, and without a sex drive." Understandably frustrated, these clients came to our medical weight-loss clinic to find out what to do next.

I wondered whether low-carbohydrate dieting was causing depression. How did lowering carbohydrate intake influence mood, appetite, cravings, and sex drive?

When I studied the most recent medical research on dieting, the answer became crystal clear. Even though women were successful losing weight on these diets, they unknowingly depleted a vital brain chemical called serotonin. Serotonin is essential for feeling happy, controlling appetite, and being interested in sex. These low-carb dieters had lost more than weight; they had also lost so much serotonin that it was affecting their brain. They desperately needed to know how to get it back.

I also found that erosion of this same neurotransmitter serotonin was responsible for setting up the yo-yo dieting cycle or spiral. Therefore, serotonin would be the answer for preventing that, too.

Like the thousands of women (and a few men) that have come through my clinic, you can learn how to recover the serotonin you lost through dieting—especially low-carb dieting. At the same time, you will discover new ways to save your serotonin and even create more.

The Feel-Good Diet plan will help you lose as much weight as you want. You will lose your weight and keep your brain. This is done by simply adjusting the way you eat to increase serotonin and by improving the hormones that control your metabolism. And get this: many of you will feel better and lose more weight by exercising less.

This book is the culmination of seven years of research about the effects of dieting on brain chemistry, metabolism, and hormones. I am excited to teach you what I have learned in *The Feel-Good Diet*.

—Cheryle Hart, M.D.

Introduction

Have you been on at least five diets in the past fifteen years?

Do you crave carbohydrates, especially in the afternoon or evening?

Is chocolate your downfall?

Do you think a lot about food?

Do you reach for certain foods when you are stressed?

Do you fall off your diet when you start feeling deprived?

Do you give up because you feel your willpower is not strong enough?

Have you ever been doing great on your diet but quit because it got boring?

Do you regain even more weight after dieting?

These are all signs of a depleted-brain-hormone condition we call "yo-yo brain," caused by repeated yo-yo dieting. Women older than forty who are stressed out are the most vulnerable to developing yo-yo brain. Those with depression, chronic fatigue, fibromyalgia, winter "blues," premenstrual syndrome (PMS), and hormone imbalances of menopause are also prime targets for developing serotonin depletion.

Recently, experts have identified that frequent or cyclic (yo-yo) dieting results in depletions of brain hormones, called neurotransmitters. These chemical regulators are necessary for controlling your appetite, cravings, mood, energy, metabolism, and sex drive. Serotonin, one of the most important neurotransmitters, is continuously lost during yo-yo dieting. While most dieters fixate on how many pounds they are losing, few realize that they are also losing important neurotransmitters. More important, they don't realize that they can prevent that loss.

Just imagine the life you could live if you could:

- Stop thinking about food so much
- Eat smaller portions
- Feel less hungry
- Have more energy
- Stop craving the foods that "do you in"
- Stop feeling deprived
- Maintain your new weight

According to a Mayo Clinic diet report, 40 percent of dieters quit within the first month of starting a diet. Two-thirds never make it past three months. The reasons for "giving up" included losing willpower, feeling deprived, being too hungry, having strong cravings, and feeling too stressed or too tired. Every one of these occurs because of serotonin depletion due to yo-yo brain.

Women are especially at risk for developing yo-yo brain. Recent medical studies from Massachusetts Institute of Technology (MIT), Harvard, and Oxford show that within the first three weeks of being on any diet, women start depleting their serotonin. (Men showed less of a serotonin drop.) The more a woman diets, the more her serotonin drops. This shows up as low motivation, loss of focus, weak willpower, drained energy, increased fatigue, bad moods, challenging cravings, and increased appetite.

Are men different from women when it comes to dieting and serotonin depletion? Brain imaging studies reveal that the brain chemistry of dieting women differs from that of dieting men. This means that diets that work for men may actually be harmful to women. Not many people are aware of this important new medical finding.

Many serotonin-depleted women have been on the popular low-carbohydrate diets. While these diets claim to have many health benefits, they fail to mention the negative effects they have on lowering serotonin.

Our book tells you the whole story about the serotonin-dieting connection—what it is, why it occurs, and how it affects your appetite, cravings, mood, willpower, energy, metabolism, and sex drive. Most important, we tell you how to recover by rebuilding your serotonin and other important neurotransmitters.

The Feel-Good Diet plan combines the nutritional, hormonal, and activity basics necessary to lose and successfully maintain weight more easily. Up until now, diets have not supported the most critical links for long-term weight maintenance—the brain hormones known as neurotransmitters. Restoring and balancing your neurotransmitters are the keys to your success.

Most diets are based on "eating less and exercising more." It's no wonder they ultimately fail. Restriction of certain foods and excessive exercise actually deplete valuable brain hormones. Once you know how to support your neurotransmitters, you will be rewarded with easier, quicker, and better weight-loss results. More important, your mood, energy, and sex drive will be substantially improved with the Feel-Good Diet.

This four-part method enables you to lose weight and maintain it without disrupting the brain-serotonin connection. It has been successful with thousands of our weight-loss clinic patients over the past six years. They report feeling "better than they can ever remember."

How to Use This Book

In Part I, What Happens to Your Brain Hormones When You Diet, you'll learn what neurotransmitters are, how they work in the brain, and how to tell if you are deficient in them. You'll also learn how hormones affect your appetite and weight loss and how they interact with neurotransmitters.

Part II, The Feel-Good Weight-Loss Program, describes the four steps needed to optimize your brain hormones. First we go through each step separately. Then we connect them so that you can follow one simple program.

These four action steps are:

1. Nutritional ways to support neurotransmitters
2. Neurotransmitter supplement therapy
3. Increasing metabolism and energy
4. Neurotransmitter boosting with exercise and other activities

Some people like to know how the clock works, but others just want to know what time it is. We wrote this book with both of you in mind. Part I describes "how the clock works." You can go directly to Part II if you are ready to know "what time it is." In other words, you realize that your neurotransmitters are deficient and you want to do something about it right now.

So cut the string to your yo-yo diet . . . let's begin.

What Happens to Your Brain Hormones When You Diet

1

Dieting to Lose . . . Serotonin?

We all start with an ample supply of more than two hundred different brain messengers called neurotransmitters. Serotonin is the most well known of these and in many ways the most important one for controlling our mood, food, and attitude. As we grow older, our supply of serotonin drops. Stress, hormone changes, excess caffeine, nicotine, alcohol, certain medications, and environmental toxins can also use it up. But the most common drain of serotonin is repeated cyclic or "yo-yo dieting," resulting in what we call "yo-yo brain."

High-protein diets that severely restrict carbohydrates, such as the South Beach Diet and Atkins, work by controlling the fat-making hormone insulin. As effective as these diets are for weight loss, they drastically lower the important brain hormone serotonin. This negatively affects your mood and increases your appetite and cravings. For reasons explained in Chapter 4, women (as compared to men)— even those who are dieting for the first time—are especially prone to serotonin depletion during low-carb dieting. Physicians have reported cases of women having significant personality changes while being on low-carbohydrate diets. They recovered once they started eating carbohydrates again.

Two stories from clients at our clinic highlight the problems that occur when you lose serotonin and how the Feel-Good Diet Program was used. The first case shows what happens during yo-yo dieting. The second case illustrates what can happen to a dedicated low-carb dieter.

Mary H.—a Yo-Yo Dieter

Mary H., age fifty-seven, bounced into the interview room at a full five feet four inches tall. She had just lost twenty pounds in just two months—down from 219 to 199 pounds. She was a library researcher at a local high school. The stress of her job seemed to require midday snacks for comfort. After dinner each evening she would sit with her husband watching television and continue snacking. Her husband, a slim, athletic man, was the type who munched throughout the day until he fell asleep at night. "Why is it so many men can eat so much and not gain weight?" she wondered.

Upon further reflection, she realized that her husband had an active job and exercised every evening with a five-mile run. She sat at a desk all day and ate rich and sugary carbs for comfort. Rarely could she find the energy to take a walk around the block.

Mary had tried so many diets throughout the years. She always did great at first, but by the third week she would sink into depression. She ate more and snacked more so her weight went back up. As each diet struggle continued, she was barely able to drag herself through the day. She dreaded going to those weight-loss meetings, which were supposed to inspire her.

"After all," she sighed, "I ate their food and was supposed to be losing weight. But I wasn't. I started gaining." After a short pause, she admitted that even though she was eating their food, she also continued with all the snacks that brought her comfort through the years: doughnuts, peanut butter, and sugary snacks. She ate most of these near the end of the day while at work. After dinner, she continued snacking with her husband right through the evening.

"I didn't admit to my support group that I was eating all that stuff. I was too embarrassed. Finally, I just couldn't go back. I worried that someone would notice I was gaining and accuse me of cheating. So I would drop out, typically with more weight than when I started." She felt totally defeated and was more depressed than ever.

"No diet has ever worked for me," she told us. "Even when I eat the foods I'm supposed to, something always seems to happen. I get tired, I get depressed, and I get irritable. I sit beside my husband, who is snacking and not gaining, and I hate him. I can barely drag myself out of bed. I don't know why."

After years of frustration, Mary decided to try losing weight one more time. Seeing how well her friend did on our program, Mary registered at our clinic. Many weeks later she admitted to us that she had been so discouraged from her past dieting experiences that she really hadn't expected to lose weight.

But this time would be different. When Mary started our program, she learned a whole new approach to choosing her foods that enabled her to lose weight while maintaining her mood. She also learned the importance of using natural neurotransmitter supplements.

She was really impressed when she starting losing weight after the first week. For the first time in years, she had enough energy to go on a walk. Best of all, at about week four—fully expecting to "hit the wall"—she was amazed when a slowdown didn't happen. She just continued to take off the pounds.

"This is the first diet that I have been on where depression never hit, I didn't suffer from insomnia, nor was I craving the sweets." In fact, by week eight, she was on cloud nine, exclaiming, "Life is great when you get a good night's sleep."

By the ninth week she was walking two miles a day. "I have so much energy now, and I can't figure it out. But I'm losing weight,

I have no cravings, I'm sleeping, and I feel great. I am surprised how easy it has been to give up snacking in the afternoon. I actually enjoy sitting with my husband in the evening, even when he snacks." About the improvement in her mood she remarked, "I hosted a family reunion this summer with thirty-six people in my house, and I didn't snap at one person."

Though Mary had lost weight "about a million times before," something was very different this time. She could credit her new experience only to the fact that she was learning to pay attention to her brain chemistry. "Neurotransmitter support doesn't make you feel high or as if you are on medicine. It lets you feel like you are supposed to feel—alive, happy, and willing to live your life fully. I can now choose foods that I know are good for me and will help me lose weight while I keep my sanity."

Marcia L.—Lost Weight but Felt Awful

Marcia liked to do things on her own, including losing weight. She jumped full force onto the low-carb diet bandwagon that everyone was on at the office. Thirty-six pounds later, friends couldn't believe how great Marcia looked. In fact, she swore she hadn't had one piece of bread or a potato in eight months.

At her annual exam at our office, we commented on how much weight she lost since she had last been in. "Trouble is," she admitted, "I thought I was going to feel happier." Instead she was feeling more and more tired. She wondered if she might even be depressed. Moreover, she sensed that she was worrying a lot more about things. Her husband called to say that he was concerned about her emotional state. She was more irritable and overly critical about things that never used to bother her. "Especially weird," he reported, "is that she is compulsive about having things organized in even numbers." In fact, she had to count her ice cubes in her drinks to be sure there was an even amount.

She admitted that she had followed a very low-carbohydrate diet exactly to a tee, never cheating once. With her symptoms of depression, anxiety, irritability, and compulsive mannerisms, we realized that Marcia was suffering from severe serotonin depletion. Her strict limiting of carbohydrates needed for serotonin caused this.

Marcia was so resistant to bringing carbohydrates back into her diet that she insisted on first trying a prescription medication to boost her serotonin. After two months, she reported that she felt better emotionally, but the medication interfered with her sex drive. This was such a serious problem that her husband came along to her next appointment.

She said that she wanted to feel like her old self again, especially sexually. We insisted that she would need to discontinue her prescription medication and learn how to raise her serotonin level naturally, through diet and supplements. Realizing that her marriage was in jeopardy, she agreed to try the plan for one month.

In just four weeks on our program, she went off the medication without any problems. She maintained her weight while eating bread and potatoes once again. Feeling great, she was back to enjoying a healthy sexual relationship with her husband.

Marcia's case is extreme, yet her experience is not unusual. During the latest low-carb diet trend over the past ten years, we have noticed that physicians have increased the number of new prescriptions for antidepressants to women who are dieting. This is not surprising because the research shows that serotonin is depleted with low-carb diets.

Dieting and Serotonin

Of course, some women are more prone to these symptoms than others. Women at greatest risk for serotonin deficiency are those who already have problems with their mood, appetite, and sleep. Hormone imbalances make women even more vulnerable to depleting their serotonin. These often occur during the monthly premenstrual cycle (PMS), with pregnancy, and during menopause.

Stress also uses up a lot of serotonin. Women under stress who are also trying to lose weight are more likely to have serotonin-related problems. These show up as depression, panic attacks, anxiety, irritability, insomnia, migraine headaches, fibromyalgia, compulsive overeating, bulimia, and excessive cravings for carbohydrates, chocolate, caffeine, alcohol, or nicotine.

How do antidepressants boost serotonin? Women with low-serotonin symptoms are often prescribed one of the popular antidepressant medications called SSRIs (selective serotonin reuptake inhibitors). These medications help you preserve your existing serotonin. They act by keeping serotonin active in your brain longer. They do not actually help you make more. Prozac (fluoxetine) was the first SSRI on the market, and many others are now available. Common brand names include Paxil, Zoloft, Celexa, and Lexapro. Even though SSRIs have vastly improved and even saved the lives of millions, they do have side effects, some of which can be fatal. A frustrating yet common drawback of SSRIs is that they can drastically dampen your sex drive. Understandably, this can seriously impact intimate relationships. So, while these SSRIs will treat your symptoms, they will not help you make more serotonin.

Fortunately, there are other ways besides medications that can help you improve your serotonin levels. The types of food you eat, the supplements you take, and the exercises and activities you do all can help you recover your serotonin.

In the rest of Part I, you'll learn how neurotransmitters work. You will understand how mood, energy, appetite, and sex drive are controlled by your brain chemistry.

Main Points in Chapter 1

- Low-carbohydrate, high-protein diets actually lead to serotonin depletion, especially in women.
- Serotonin regulates your mood, appetite, cravings, sleep, and sex drive.

2

The Brain's Messengers: Neurotransmitters

Neurotransmitters are the small chemical messengers that let various parts of the brain communicate with each other and with the rest of the body. Sometimes they are referred to as brain hormones.

The Austrian scientist Otto Loewi discovered the first neurotransmitter in 1921. In the past twenty years, more than two hundred neurotransmitters have been identified. They are responsible for all of our thoughts, moods, and feelings. They control our energy level, appetite, and which foods we crave. Neurotransmitters regulate how well we sleep and even our interest in sex. Each neurotransmitter affects these differently. Some neurotransmitters excite the brain, while others act as inhibitors. For instance, dopamine raises energy while serotonin is calming. Proper *amounts* and *proportions* of neurotransmitters are necessary for achieving and maintaining physical and emotional health.

Here are some of the most studied neurotransmitters affecting mood, appetite, and energy:

- **Serotonin—*the calming neurotransmitter***: *Serotonin* improves your sense of well-being, controls your cravings, helps you feel satisfied after eating, and helps you sleep and calms your mind.
- **Catecholamines—*the energizing neurotransmitters***: *Dopamine* raises excitement, stimulates anticipation of being rewarded, improves brain and muscle energy, and makes you feel sexy. *Norepinephrine* increases metabolism and triggers a "fight-or-flight" response to immediate stress. It is produced from dopamine. *Epinephrine* signals a full-body reaction to danger, fear, and stress. It is commonly called *adrenaline*.
- **Endorphins—*natural painkillers***: Endorphins provide pain relief and at high levels cause euphoria.
- **Glutamine—*muscle energizer***: Glutamine lowers blood sugar (glucose) by storing it as glycogen in muscles during exercise. It also helps support your immune system.
- **Gamma-aminobutyric acid (GABA)—*natural tranquilizer***: GABA relieves anxiety, relaxes muscles, and enhances sleep.
- **Glutamate—*brain sugar regulator***: Glutamate carries glucose into the cells of the brain and stimulates brain activity.

How Neurotransmitters Work

Neurotransmitters are produced and stored in brain cells, called *neurons*. The brain is made up of billions of neurons that look and act differently from any other type of cell. Resembling a tree, they have a long trunk (*axon*) extending out from a central round body (cell body) with smaller branches (*dendrites*) jutting out from the cell body. (See Figure 2.1.) The outstretched dendrites reach over to each other, allowing many cells to communicate with each other at the same time. Dendrites do not ever touch each other but are separated by a tiny gap called the *synaptic space*.

FIGURE 2.1 Nerve Cell "Neuron"

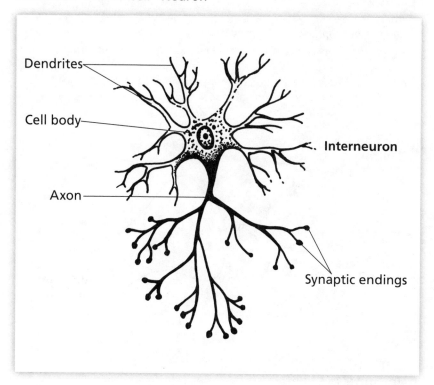

Neurotransmitters are produced and stored in tiny bubble-like vesicles at the tip of each dendrite. Messages pass between dendrites by a unique combination of neurotransmitters, electricity, and chemistry. (See Figure 2.2.) When an electrical current starts in a neuron, it spreads out to the vesicles at the very ends of the dendrite branches. Vesicles then spill their neurotransmitters out into the synaptic space. The neurotransmitters drift through the synaptic space and attach onto neighboring neurons at docking sites called *receptors*. Each neurotransmitter has its own type of receptor. When the receptors are stimulated by enough neurotransmitters, the signal transmits through the brain and out to the body at lightning speeds. Once transmission has been made, the receptors release the neurotransmitters, and they are reabsorbed by the original neuron.

FIGURE 2.2 "Talking Neurons"

1. After being electrically stimulated, the released neurotransmitter molecules drift out into a space between neurons, called the "synaptic space."
2. Neurotransmitters attach onto adjacent brain cells at special sites called receptors.
3. Occupied receptors activate their receiving neuron, allowing the electrical stimulation to continue on to the next brain cell.

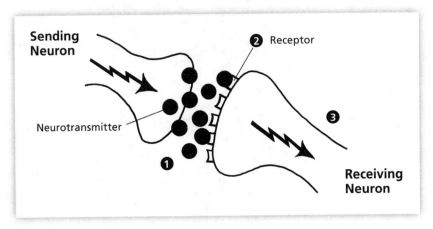

Main Points in Chapter 2

- Neurotransmitters are the messengers of the brain, sometimes referred to as brain hormones.
- Proper *amounts* and *proportions* of neurotransmitters are necessary for excellent physical and emotional health.
- Neurotransmitters are produced and stored in brain cells called neurons.
- Neurotransmitters attach to receptors to send out their messages.
- Neurotransmitters work by activating their particular receptor sites.

3

Neurotransmitters That Affect Appetite

Out of the hundreds of known neurotransmitters, only five of them have been found to have a major effect on appetite. Serotonin and dopamine are strongly involved with our eating habits. Much has been discovered about how they work together. The lesser-known glutamate/glutamine/GABA inter-relationship is becoming the focus of new research on appetite.

Serotonin

More has been written about serotonin than about any other neu-rotransmitter. Serotonin is found throughout the body; the diges-tive system contains 90 percent, with the remainder found in blood vessels and the brain. It plays an important role in regulating your memory, learning, appetite, blood pressure, and body temperature. Serotonin in the brain influences your state of mind, your desires for carbohydrates, and your response to situations that make you frus-trated or angry; it even influences your interest in sex.

Serotonin is essential for your sense of well-being—what is known as "being in a good mood." Low serotonin levels cause insomnia and depression, eating disorders, cravings, aggressive behavior, and increased sensitivity to pain, and they are associated with obsessive-compulsive conditions.

Serotonin is made in two steps starting with the amino acid *tryptophan*. Amino acids are the small building blocks of protein. Tryptophan is the least abundant of all of the twenty-two amino acids found in protein. Each step in making serotonin needs vitamins C, B_1, B_6, and folic acid as well as the minerals magnesium, calcium, and zinc. These vitamins and minerals are called *cofactors*. With the help of these cofactors, tryptophan first converts to 5-hydroxytryptophan (5-HTP) and then to serotonin. Some serotonin goes on to make melatonin, the hormone that is needed for sleep. (See Figure 3.1.)

FIGURE 3.1   Making Serotonin

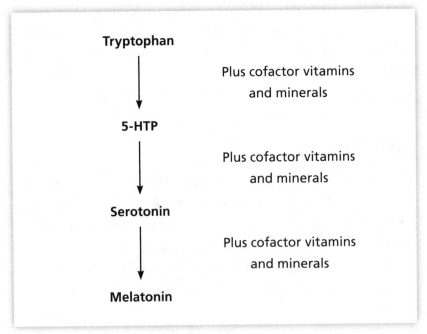

Tryptophan

Plus cofactor vitamins and minerals

5-HTP

Plus cofactor vitamins and minerals

Serotonin

Plus cofactor vitamins and minerals

Melatonin

Dopamine and the Catecholamines

Catecholamines are a family of energizing neurotransmitters. They are made in the brain and in the adrenal glands. They come from the amino acids *tyrosine* and *phenylalanine*. These are two of the most abundant amino acids found in protein. Catecholamines include dopamine, norepinephrine, and epinephrine—sometimes called adrenaline. (See Figure 3.2.)

Catecholamines work together so you can react to urgent situations needing immediate coordination among your muscles, brain, and central nervous system. Dopamine rapidly converts

FIGURE 3.2 Making Catecholamines: Dopamine, Norepinephrine, and Epinephrine

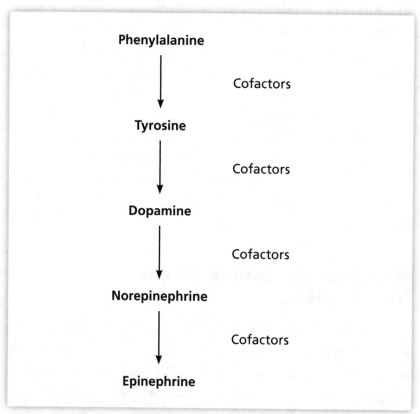

to norepinephrine and epinephrine when your brain senses danger or when you feel fear. The primal "fight-or-flight" response to these situations automatically activates your catecholamine neurotransmitters.

Dopamine makes you more alert and focused, increasing your ability to learn and remember. After achieving an important goal, the "pleasure center" of your brain is flooded by dopamine. This gives you the feelings of elation and accomplishment. Dopamine is also activated when you anticipate eating or even thinking about having sex. Thrill-seeking activities stimulate dopamine release. Due to their effects on your brain, catecholamines are the chemicals most associated with addictive behaviors.

Norepinephrine, also called noradrenaline, is the neurotransmitter needed for increased motivation, alertness, and concentration. It helps form new memories in the brain and stores them long term. Norepinephrine also increases your metabolic rate.

Epinephrine helps you react to sudden, unexpected stimuli such as gunshots, screeching tires, yelling, and even thunder. It is also released when you are under stress. Epinephrine constricts your blood vessels and raises your heart rate, breathing rate, and blood pressure. These emergency responses happen automatically and are necessary short-term reactions to danger. However, prolonged physical or emotional stress makes your body feel constantly threatened and requires more epinephrine. Because epinephrine is made from dopamine, long-term stress will lower your dopamine levels.

How Serotonin and Dopamine Work Together

Serotonin and dopamine work together to create balance in your moods, desires, and sense of well-being (see Table 3.1). They cause your brain to respond to situations in opposite but complementary ways. Serotonin is soothing, while dopamine is stimulating. Serotonin is relaxing, while dopamine is energizing. Serotonin signals that everything is all right, while dopamine alerts you to take notice of what is going on. You can see why it is important to have both of these in adequate, balanced amounts.

TABLE 3.1 Serotonin vs. Dopamine Effects

WHAT SEROTONIN DOES	WHAT DOPAMINE DOES
Calms	Energizes
Promotes positive feelings of well-being	Increases motivation and ambition
Signals fullness when eating (satiety)	Signals hunger (like an on/off switch)
Provides serenity and "afterglow" following sex	Promotes sexual desires, arousal, and climax
THINGS THAT BOOST SEROTONIN LEVELS	**THINGS THAT BOOST DOPAMINE LEVELS**
Eating carbohydrates, especially sweet or starchy ones	Drinking or eating foods high in caffeine
Repetitive "crunching" or chewing, such as grazing on carrots, sunflower seeds, gum	Eating chocolate
Listening to soft music or new age music	Listening and/or dancing to loud, fast music with a strong bass sound
Meditating	Drumming
Taking baths	Taking showers
Silent praying	Gospel singing
Slow dancing	Fast, rhythmic dancing, such as rock and roll
Laughing	Laughing
Using nicotine	Going on thrill rides; driving fast
"Comfort" eating	Smelling or seeing delectable foods
Feeling tired when drinking alcohol	The "buzz" feeling when drinking alcohol
Yoga	Watching or participating in competitive sports
Massage	Exercising
Hugging and caressing	Anticipating fun or exciting events like parties or vacations

Serotonin and dopamine work together in the hypothalamic area of the brain to regulate food intake. Dopamine rises with the anticipation of eating and peaks as you start to eat. This dopamine peak causes the release of serotonin, which signals satiety, the feeling of fullness, and you naturally stop eating.

Recent research shows that the formation of serotonin in the brain competes with production of dopamine. Whether you make serotonin or dopamine depends on which amino acids are the most abundant in your brain. Tryptophan makes serotonin. Tyrosine and phenylalanine produce dopamine. Because protein foods naturally contain more tyrosine and phenylalanine than tryptophan, high-protein diets produce more dopamine than serotonin. Tryptophan, however, has its own strategy for eventually getting into the brain to make serotonin. This requires help from carbohydrates. Chapter 6, Insulin Resistance and Serotonin, explains how this happens.

Many disorders are caused by deficiencies and imbalances in serotonin and dopamine. These conditions include depression, anxiety, chronic fatigue, fibromyalgia, headaches, premenstrual syndrome, appetite and eating disorders, addictions, attention deficit disorders, chronic pain, insomnia, irritability and anger disorders, low motivation, and decreased sex desire. To avoid these problems, it is critical to balance enough serotonin with dopamine.

Other Appetite-Affecting Neurotransmitters

Even though the focus of the book is on serotonin and its complementary neurotransmitter dopamine, other neurotransmitters have been studied as they relate to your appetite and behavior. At this time the details of how they work in the brain are not as well understood.

- **GABA**, chemically known as gamma-aminobutyric acid, is considered an "inhibitory" neurotransmitter. It slows down the synapses in your brain, so they can hear other neurotransmitters.

GABA is less understood than serotonin, but it seems to play a similar role in regulating your mood.

- **Glutamate** is an activating neurotransmitter similar to dopamine. It works with GABA in the same way dopamine works with serotonin. While GABA calms brain activity, glutamate stimulates it. Glutamate helps transport sugar into the brain and is essential for thinking and feeling.

- **Glutamine** is the precursor amino acid for making both glutamate and GABA. The brain controls the ratio of glutamate to GABA by regulating which pathway the glutamine will take.

Main Points in Chapter 3

- Serotonin is the main neurotransmitter that controls your mood, appetite, sleep, and cravings.
- Serotonin is calming; catecholamines are stimulating.
- Both serotonin and catecholamines need to be produced in the right amounts in order to balance out their effects.
- GABA, glutamate, and glutamine also are important in controlling appetite but are less well understood.

4

Do You Have a Neurotransmitter Deficiency? Why It Happens

If there are not enough neurotransmitters available to "talk" to neurons or when the receptors are not receiving and transmitting properly, the brain message is weak. The signs and symptoms of neurotransmitter deficiencies then show up.

Neurotransmitter levels can be measured by laboratory testing. However, you can easily identify signs of deficiencies by the symptoms they cause. Your mood, energy, appetite, and cravings give important clues. For example, cravings for starchy or sugary carbohydrates or chocolate indicate you are low in serotonin. The times of the day you crave certain foods also point to a serotonin or dopamine deficiency. Tables 4.1 and 4.2 help you identify common neurotrans-

TABLE 4.1 Effects of Low Dopamine and Catecholamines

DEFICIENCY SYMPTOMS	RELATED CRAVINGS
Do You Often:	Do You Often Have Strong Desires for:
Feel low in mood or depressed?	Caffeine?
Lack energy?	Tobacco?
Lack drive or motivation?	Stimulant drugs or medications?
Lack focus or concentration?	Chocolate?
Have headaches?	
Have weak muscles?	
Have an attention deficit disorder (ADD)?	
Have chronic fatigue?	

mitter deficiencies and whether your serotonin is properly balanced with dopamine.

Common Causes of Low Levels of Serotonin and Dopamine

If you noticed familiar symptoms, there can be several causes for your levels being low.

- **Getting older.** Serotonin and dopamine are the most sensitive neurotransmitters to aging. Past age forty, 60 percent of *all adults* have some degree of neurotransmitter deficiency. As neurons age, they make fewer of these neurotransmitters. Their receptors also lose the ability to respond. A study by Carolyn Meltzer, M.D., from the University of Pittsburgh, reported a 55 percent decline in serotonin receptors due to aging. Dopamine receptors also decline as we age. Researchers noted a 6 percent decrease

TABLE 4.2 Effects of Low Serotonin

DEFICIENCY SYMPTOMS	RELATED CRAVINGS
Do You Often:	**Do You Often Have Strong Desires for:**
Feel negative or hopeless?	Sugary foods?
Feel overly worried or anxious?	Starches such as breads, pasta, rice, and potatoes?
Feel worthless?	Chocolate?
Have obsessive thoughts or behaviors?	Tobacco?
Have increased fears?	Carbohydrates in the afternoon or evening, even if you're not hungry?
Feel full after you eat but not satisfied?	Sweets, cereal, or other carbohydrates during the middle of the night?
Eat large food portions?	
Think a lot about food?	
Have afternoon or evening cravings?	
Eat when emotionally stressed?	
Feel "blue" in the winter?	
Have menstrual cycle mood shifts?	
Get easily irritated or mad?	
Have heat intolerance?	
Have panic attacks or phobias?	
Have fibromyalgia or achy muscles?	
Have TMJ (temporomandibular) joint pain or jaw clenching?	
Have chronic fatigue or chronic pain?	
Have problems sleeping, especially staying asleep?	

per decade in dopamine receptors after age twenty. This translates into decreased brain activity, deterioration in the ability to reason, and slower reaction time as we age.

- **Gender differences.** Women have one-third less serotonin than men do because men have more muscle mass; this is explained in Chapter 6, Insulin Resistance and Serotonin. Low serotonin puts women at risk for developing more problems with their moods, sleep, appetite, cravings, and willpower than men. The normal changes of women's hormones during the month also affect serotonin levels. Approximately two weeks before the menstrual cycle, serotonin levels normally drop. When ovarian hormones decline during menopause, serotonin levels also fall.

- **Prolonged emotional or physical stress.** Your body relies on the catecholamine neurotransmitters to help you cope with stress. The hormones from the "fight-or-flight" adrenal glands signal catecholamine release so that you can quickly respond. When stress is severe or prolonged, the adrenal glands eventually become exhausted and cannot keep up. This results in dopamine depletion, upsetting the delicate serotonin/dopamine balance.

- **Dieting too much.** This is the most common drain on neurotransmitters and the focus of this book. When cutting back on calories during dieting, you also restrict important nutrients. This results in neurotransmitter deficiencies. Serotonin is especially sensitive to the effects of dieting. You must intentionally support your neurotransmitters while dieting, or you will lose your willpower, develop rebound appetite and craving problems, wreck your metabolism, and fall into the vicious cycle of yo-yo dieting. Following the recommendations made in Chapter 7 will help you avoid this common dieting trap.

- **Hormone imbalances.** Hormones influence neurotransmitter release and activity. They include estrogen, progesterone, testosterone, thyroid, adrenals, and insulin. Imbalances commonly occur premenstrually, with menopause, and during times of stress. When hormones are off balance, neurotransmitters do not function well. This affects mood, energy, weight, sleep, and sexual desire. In Chapters 5 and 6 we discuss hormone effects on neurotransmitters in more detail.

- **Sleeping poorly.** Neurotransmitters affect how well you sleep. Melatonin, the sleep hormone, is made from serotonin. If your serotonin is low, you may also have sleeping problems from low melatonin. This becomes a vicious cycle, because most serotonin is replenished while you sleep.

- **Certain medications.** Long-term use of diet pills, stimulants, pain pills, and narcotics can deplete neurotransmitter stores. The diet pill combination fen-phen worked because it caused the neurons to release large amounts of appetite-suppressing dopamine and serotonin. Other diet pills containing stimulants, such as large doses of caffeine, similarly force the release of large amounts of dopamine and norepinephrine. Long-term use of these, however, causes depletions of neurotransmitters. This results in profound rebound appetite and mood problems for many dieters, especially women.

- **Exposure to neurotoxins.** Heavy metals, chemical pesticides, fertilizers, certain cleaning agents, industrial solvents, and recreational drugs can be neurotoxic, causing damage to the neurons. Neurotransmitter production and receptor activity becomes compromised.

Having too much caffeine, nicotine, and alcohol can also be neurotoxic. How much is too much?

- **Caffeine.** In addition to coffee and tea, caffeine shows up in many forms. Large amounts are often added to energy drinks, diet pills, and stimulant-type supplements. Small amounts of caffeine (25 to 75 mg a day) actually increase production of catecholamines. However, caffeine amounts of more than 100 milligrams per day have been shown to reduce production of catecholamines. This equals about three cups of drip-style coffee. A two-shot espresso contains 150 milligrams.

- **Nicotine.** Smoking more than five cigarettes a day affects neurotransmitter production. This amount of nicotine interferes with the ability of the brain to make serotonin and decrease the uptake of serotonin into the neurons. Since these receptors are being "starved" for serotonin, they signal the brain to produce more. This delayed surging of serotonin produces a calming effect a little while after smoking, which can become addictive. Nicotine also overstimulates the production of dopamine so that it desensitizes the dopamine receptors in the brain. Since it takes more and more dopamine to create the same stimulating response, nicotine becomes addictive in this way too.

- **Alcohol.** Drinking more than eight ounces of wine, sixteen ounces of beer, or two ounces of hard liquor per day affects your neurotransmitter production. Alcohol affects the production of dopamine and serotonin in a very complicated way, which also involves GABA and glutamine. Interestingly, the net effect is similar to that of nicotine. Over several weeks, constant consumption of alcohol increases the production of dopamine and decreases serotonin.

- **Recreational drugs.** The street drug Ecstasy is particularly toxic to women. It has such a strong serotonin-releasing effect that it can drain large amounts of serotonin in a very short time. Ecstasy users first report an overwhelming surge of total well-being only to plummet into feelings of despair. For young women, this is a special concern, because they are the most common users of Ecstasy. Studies report permanent damage to the serotonin receptors in the brain. Due to using Ecstasy, even strong antidepressant medications cannot restore their serotonin levels.

- **A family predisposition.** Some people inherit an inability to make enough neurotransmitters. They first experience symptoms as children or young adults. As they get older, they develop even more profound and debilitating symptoms. They often have relatives who suffer from significant emotional conditions, such as severe depression or bipolar disorders.

- **Unknown causes.** Parkinson's disease is a specific kind of dopamine deficiency. People with Parkinson's disease lose the ability to make and respond to dopamine in the part of the brain responsible for fine muscle coordination. Attention deficit disorders are due to the lack of focus that occurs with low dopamine. Hyperactivity is caused by the brain seeking to create more dopamine. Gambling, alcoholism, and other addictive behaviors are also being studied as conditions of low dopamine.

Neurotransmitter deficiencies often occur as the brain's response to our "overdoing" a good thing. Overconsumption of nicotine, alcohol, caffeine, and even food can lead to long-term shortages of serotonin and cause addictions to stimulants that produce dopamine. Environmental and genetic factors can further complicate the situation.

Main Points in Chapter 4

- Neurotransmitter deficiencies can be recognized by the specific symptoms they cause.
- Causes of neurotransmitter deficiencies include aging, being a woman, stress, dieting, hormone imbalances, lack of sleep, certain medications, neurotoxic chemicals, and heredity.

5

Hormones That Affect Neurotransmitters

Hormones are chemical messengers that are naturally secreted into your blood. They are made in specialized organs called glands. Even though each hormone carries its own set of messages throughout your body, many share similar jobs and work together. Hormones influence the neurotransmitters, whose important roles are covered in the preceding chapters. Hormones affect how well neurotransmitters are able to do their jobs. If your hormones are not balanced, then many of your body and brain functions suffer. The most important hormones affected by dieting are estrogen, progesterone, thyroid, testosterone, cortisol, and insulin. (See Figure 5.1.) These are the main hormones that influence your mood, energy, and appetite. How you eat can strongly affect them, so it's worth understanding how they work.

FIGURE 5.1   Diagram of Endocrine System

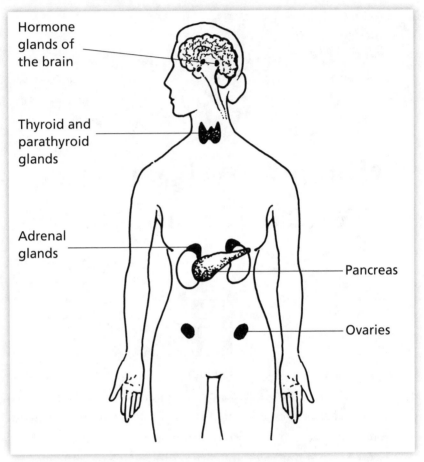

Hormone glands of the brain

Thyroid and parathyroid glands

Adrenal glands

Pancreas

Ovaries

Estrogen and Progesterone: The Female Hormones

Modern techniques of brain imaging now allow researchers to watch the brain in action. These studies reveal that the sex gland hormones estrogen, progesterone, and testosterone are perhaps the most powerful brain messengers of all. This has significant implications for women, who normally experience profound shifts of these hormones with their menstrual cycles, during pregnancy, and at menopause.

The Estrogens

The estrogen hormones are secreted by the ovaries. Men also make small amounts of estrogen through conversion of some of their testosterone. Adipose tissue (fat stores) also produces estrogen in both women and men. Estrogen protects against heart disease, stroke, osteoporosis, Alzheimer's disease, and memory disorders. It supports the health of the vaginal and bladder walls to protect against atrophy (thinning), vaginal and urinary tract infections, and urinary leakage (incontinence). Estrogen prevents symptoms of menopause including hot flashes, night sweats, and insomnia. Decreased amounts of estrogen show up as saggy breast skin, increased face wrinkles, decreased energy, depression, mood swings, and lowered sex drive (libido). Replacing estrogen during menopause has been a successful treatment for more than fifty years.

Estrogen and the Brain

Estrogen increases blood flow throughout the brain. Postmenopausal women who do not use estrogen replacement therapy show a significant decrease in brain blood flow that continues to drop over time, but estrogen therapy shows significant improvement of blood flow after only two weeks of hormone replacement. It now appears that hot flashes are not merely a benign nuisance but signal decreases in brain blood flow. The centers for memory and learning are the most affected. Based on this type of evidence, neurologists hypothesize that hot flashes contribute to degenerative aging changes in the brain, even Alzheimer's disease. In a study of 727 postmenopausal women, those not using estrogen had significantly lower scores on memory and abstract reasoning tests. These effects were reversed when they were placed on estrogen replacement therapy.

Estrogen increases levels of serotonin, dopamine, and norepinephrine. Levels of estrogen correlate positively with levels of serotonin. Serotonin is decreased in postmenopausal women, but estrogen treatment raises it to premenopausal levels.

Women taking estrogen-blocking medications, such as tamoxifen and Arimidex, exhibit greater symptoms of depression. A comprehensive review of twenty-six studies of postmenopausal women found that estrogen replacement therapy had moderate to large beneficial effects on improving depression.

Parkinson's disease is a gradually progressive neurological disorder characterized by tremor at rest, slowness of movement, and poor balance. With Parkinson's disease, dopamine-producing cells in the substantia nigra part of the brain degenerate. Symptoms usually respond to treatment with levodopa, which helps the brain make more dopamine. This works for several years, after which the disease progresses despite this therapy. Recently, estrogen has been shown to improve the action of levodopa, thereby delaying the onset of Parkinson's. Estrogen appears to protect dopamine-producing neurons from deteriorating. It also increases the receptors' sensitivity to dopamine. On average, women with low estrogen levels develop Parkinson's six years earlier and more severely than women using estrogen. Research on estrogen therapy and Parkinson's disease is in its early stages, but results are promising.

Progesterone

Progesterone is also secreted by the ovaries. It is produced only after ovulation, when an egg is released from the ovary. During the reproductive years, progesterone's main job is to help the body prepare for and support a pregnancy. After menopause, when the ability to reproduce ceases, treating women with progesterone helps protect them against uterine and breast cancers, osteoporosis, fibrocystic breast disease, and ovarian cysts. For the past thirty years, most physicians have prescribed a synthetic progesterone called medroxyprogesterone or progestin. These synthetic forms have been associated with side effects such as bloating, headaches, fatigue, depression, and weight gain. The results of the 2003 WHI Study (Women's Health Initiative Study) raised serious concerns about the association of synthetic progestins with an increased risk of breast cancer, heart attack, stroke, and blood clotting complications. Recently, natural progesterone derived from plants has become widely available. These have fewer side effects than the synthetic progestins.

Progesterone and Neurotransmitters

During childbearing years, the ovaries secrete progesterone after ovulation. This occurs cyclically two weeks out of each menstrual month. Progesterone's main functions are to prepare the uterus for pregnancy and sustain the pregnancy to term. Women who do not ovulate, who are in menopause, or who have had surgical removal of their ovaries do not make progesterone. Men do not make progesterone.

Researchers are not clear on the exact relationship of progesterone to neurotransmitters. But ask any woman who has had increased mood swings and chocolate cravings before her menstrual period, and you realize that progesterone must be associated somehow with serotonin. The classic symptoms of PMS are the same as those of serotonin deficiency. These shared symptoms include depressed mood, irritability, anger, aggression, poor impulse control, increased appetite, and cravings for salty or sugary carbohydrates. Over the years, PMS treatments were mainly aimed at adjusting progesterone levels using oral contraceptives, progesterone pills and creams, vitamins, minerals, and herbs. The results were not very consistent. Treatments that affect serotonin levels are the most successful. The Food and Drug Administration (FDA) has approved the use of SSRIs for reducing severe PMS symptoms.

Women in their reproductive years need to pay special attention to supporting their serotonin while dieting. Willpower is most likely to weaken right after ovulation, when serotonin falls to its lowest level. This occurs during the two weeks before menstruation each month. Women placed on synthetic progestins, such as birth control pills, medroxyprogesterone (Provera), and Depo-Provera injections consistently report more problems controlling their moods, weight, appetite, and cravings. The newer bioidentical progesterone compounds appear to have less severe side effects on serotonin.

Thyroid and Testosterone: The Hormones of Metabolism

Metabolism is the measurement of how effectively you burn calories for energy. Cells burn calories in *mitochondria*, the energy factories of your body. While mitochondria are found in every cell, muscles contain the most. Therefore, the amount of muscle you have determines your metabolism. Thyroid and testosterone are the hormones that most affect your metabolism.

Thyroid

Thyroid is a metabolic hormone secreted by a butterfly-shaped gland that straddles your Adam's apple in your throat. It controls the growth and metabolism of every cell in the body. Thyroid helps regulate blood circulation, body temperature, metabolism, and brain function. It contributes to energy levels, temperature regulation, and body warmth.

Thyroid increases fat breakdown, resulting in weight loss. It protects against heart and blood vessel disease and improves brain function. Thyroid hormone is probably the safest and most beneficial cholesterol-lowering agent, yet it is infrequently used for this. Thyroid influences your heart rate and dilates blood vessels to increase blood circulation. This increases oxygen delivery to cells. With more oxygen, calories are burned faster.

The thyroid gland makes two forms of thyroid hormone: thyroxine, which is known as T-4, and thyronine, called T-3. T-4 is the one you make the most of, but it is not very strong acting. Most T-4 is kept in storage in the thyroid gland. When thyroid hormone is needed, T-4 is converted to its more potent, active T-3 form. A special converting enzyme is needed for this change to occur. About 80 percent of your total thyroid hormone stays in its inactive, stored T-4 form. Only 20 percent changes to T-3, yet it is four times stronger than T-4.

A low thyroid level is called hypothyroidism. Hashimoto's thyroiditis is an inflammatory condition of the thyroid and results in hypothyroidism. Too much thyroid hormone secretion, as is seen in Graves' disease, is called hyperthyroidism. Hyperthyroid symptoms include jitteriness, heart palpitations, heart rate irregularities, bulging eyeballs (exophthalmos), anxiety, sleeplessness, weight loss, irritability, and osteoporosis.

Hypothyroid (low) is more common, especially among women. There are more than thirty signs and symptoms of a low thyroid. They occur with either low T-4 or low T-3 levels and include the following:

- Fatigue, even in the morning after a night's sleep
- Lower-than-normal body temperature (98.6°F)
- Cold hands and feet
- Greater susceptibility to colds and other viruses
- Depression and mood swings
- Unexplained weight gain
- Thinning hair
- Loss of outer ends of eyebrow lines
- Water retention
- Puffy eyelids, especially in the morning
- Dry skin
- Headaches
- Insomnia
- High cholesterol

The thyroid gland is under the control of the pituitary, the "master gland" that is located at the base of the brain. The brain sends out a signaling hormone called TSH (thyroid-stimulating hormone) when the body needs more thyroid hormone. This signal causes T-4 production and its conversion to T-3.

Stress makes large demands on the thyroid. During acute stress, the production and secretion of T-4 and T-3 increases. These increased levels send a message back to the pituitary gland so less TSH is produced. Under prolonged stress the thyroid cannot produce enough hormones, and hypothyroid (low thyroid) symptoms occur. The pituitary reacts by increasing TSH release, which then screams out for more thyroid hormone release. The higher the TSH rises, the more depleted your thyroid gland is.

Screening lab tests usually include only TSH and T-4. These may show normal levels, yet the active T-3 could be abnormally low, especially during stress. In this case, full benefits of thyroid support may never occur unless T-3 is also supplied. If you suspect that you have low thyroid, a panel that includes TSH, free T-4, and free T-3 gives the most complete picture of your thyroid function.

Low or borderline-low levels of either T-4 or T-3 deserve to be optimized to improve your energy, weight loss, metabolism, and health. Many doctors do not supplement thyroid until your levels drop below the normal range. However, in our clinical experience, optimizing thyroid levels by keeping them in the mid to upper ranges of the normal can provide significant support of energy, weight loss, and metabolism.

Many commonly prescribed thyroid-replacement formulas contain only the T-4 component (Synthroid, Levoxyl, levothyroxine). These usually work well because our bodies will usually change T-4 to T-3 when more thyroid is needed. However, as we age past forty and during stress, less T-3 is produced. Thyroid expert Bente Appelhop recently commented in the *Journal of Clinical Endocrinology and Metabolism* that "a fair proportion of patients with hypothyroidism (low thyroid) remains with health complaints, despite substitution therapy with levothyroxine (T-4) and normalizing TSH levels.

Therefore these patients could benefit from supplementing T-3." Brands of thyroid-replacement formulas that contain T-3 include Armour and Cytomel.

Recent research supporting the use of T-3 shows:

- **Thyroid and synthetic estrogen.** Women on synthetic estrogen replacement therapy and oral contraceptives often develop T-3 deficiencies. This could explain their frequent complaints of fatigue and weight gain. Adding T-3 would remedy this.
- **Thyroid and antidepressants.** Antidepressant medications were substantially enhanced by the addition of T-3 in the treatment of post-traumatic stress disorders. Patients on lithium improved with the addition of T-3. This occurred even when subjects had normal thyroid measurements.
- **Thyroid and weight gain.** As you gain weight, your body tries to counteract the gain by increasing the use of your thyroid hormones. As you continue gaining weight, thyroid hormone levels, especially T-3, eventually become deficient. Research of body weight changes and thyroid function published by thyroid expert M. Rosenbaum shows that better weight control is achieved by supplementing with both T-4 and T-3 rather than with just T-4 alone.

Besides taking prescription thyroid hormones, you can improve the activity of your thyroid gland by doing the following:

- Include adequate amounts of the amino acid tyrosine in your diet. Tyrosine is the basic building block of all the thyroid hormones. It is abundantly available in meat, dairy, eggs, fish, and poultry.
- Include enough iodine in your diet. Iodized salt, especially sea salt, is recommended. If you routinely use iodized salt in your diet, you will get enough iodine.

- Include adequate selenium in your diet. It is an important trace mineral needed for the conversion of T-4 to its more active T-3 form. The brown skin of Brazil nuts contains the highest amounts of selenium found in foods. Each Brazil nut contains about 75 micrograms. Significant amounts of selenium are also found in tuna and cod fish. You can also buy a selenium supplement in capsule form at vitamin stores. The recommended daily dose of selenium to help convert T-4 to T-3 is 200 micrograms.
- Take supplements in the form of glandulars that contain T-4 and T-3 thyroid extract from animals. They are available at many health food stores.
- Limit your exposure to chlorine. It inactivates thyroid by blocking the places where iodine is supposed to attach.
  - Chlorine is commonly used as a water treatment chemical and is present in most municipal tap water. You can filter chlorine out of your water by using carbon filtration, reverse osmosis, and steam distillation processes.
  - Public pools and spas are required to use large amounts of chlorine to sanitize the water. Swimming in these may expose you to levels of chlorine that lower active thyroid levels.
  - One major type of plastic used in consumer products is PVC or polyvinyl chloride. Trace amounts of active chlorine remain in this plastic after it is made. When heated, even in the microwave, PVCs release chlorine. PVC plastic is found in many items, such as shower curtains, plastic tablecloths, soft baby toys, and some beverage containers. Many homes built in the 1970s and 1980s commonly used PVC water piping. Manufacturers must indicate what type of plastic they use. On beverage containers, this is coded on the bottom of the bottle. Containers made with PP (polypropylene), PC (polycarbonate), or PET or PETE (polyethylene terephthalate) plastic containers are the safest.

Testosterone

Testosterone is an important hormone secreted by the ovaries, testicles, and adrenal glands. It controls energy, muscle mass, strength, endurance, body fat, exercise tolerance, and intellectual and emotional health. Testosterone protects against cardiovascular disease (heart attacks and strokes), hypertension (high blood pressure), obesity, and arthritis. Testosterone improves lean muscle mass, increases bone density, decreases cholesterol, improves skin tone, improves healing capacity, and increases libido and sexual performance.

Testosterone's reputation mostly revolves around men's sex drive. But it is also important for metabolism in both men and women. Women are surprised to find out that their bodies make testosterone, although men make more than a hundred times more. Testosterone improves metabolism by building muscle. Testosterone has many other functions and supports women's health much the same as it does for men.

The ovaries are the main producers of testosterone in women, while the testicles produce it in men. The adrenal glands also make small amounts of testosterone. As we age past forty, a natural decline of testosterone production occurs. Stress causes the brain to produce more norepinephrine (adrenaline) and cortisol. These interact with the central nervous system to lower production and absorption of testosterone (see Cortisol later in this chapter). Because testosterone is a major factor in increasing muscle mass, this helps explain why metabolism slows down with aging and stress.

These are functions of testosterone:

- Enhancing libido
- Improving the effects of estrogen
- Strengthening bones
- Increasing lean muscle mass
- Decreasing fat stores
- Improving mood

- Increasing energy
- Promoting feelings of well-being
- Building skin collagen
- Lowering LDL ("bad") cholesterol
- Controlling blood sugar
- Strengthening tendons and ligaments

Testosterone can be measured with saliva or blood testing. Replacement of low testosterone requires a medical prescription. You can, however, increase the production of your testosterone by taking the precursor hormone, DHEA (dehydroepiandrosterone). (See DHEA later in this chapter.)

Cortisol and DHEA: The Stress Hormones

Stress is a body condition that occurs in response to actual or anticipated difficulties in life. People often experience stress as a result of major events in their lives such as marriage or loss of a job. Stress may also occur in response to daily problems such as driving in heavy traffic or being hurried by someone. In addition, people may experience stress when they perceive a threat to themselves. Causes of stress are called stressors. These are outside forces that place unusual demands on a person's body or mind.

These are some common stressors:

- Emotional triggers such as anger, fear, worry, anxiety, and guilt
- Challenging situations
- Depression
- Feeling overworked (physical or mental strain)
- Late hours/insufficient sleep
- Chronic, severe, or prolonged infections
- Surgery or injury
- Chronic inflammation, pain, or illness
- Chronic or severe allergies

- Severely restricted diets or poor nutrition
- Excessive use of stimulants such as caffeine, diet pills, or stimulant herbs

Stress sets off an alarm reaction in the body causing shifts in certain hormones and neurotransmitters. When you feel stressed, your catecholamines and serotonin quickly activate the adrenal glands. The adrenals then release hormones that enable you to react to the emergency situation. During short-term stress, adrenal hormones and neurotransmitter levels rise quickly and then return to normal when the stress subsides. Under chronic (long-term) stress, these hormones and neurotransmitters are overproduced. Levels peak and remain elevated. Eventually prolonged stress wears out production of adrenal hormones and neurotransmitters, so levels drop below normal.

The adrenal glands are small triangular glands located on top of both kidneys. They produce the stress hormones cortisol and DHEA, which do the following:

- Aid the body in coping with physical and emotional stress
- Control blood pressure, water, and electrolyte balance
- Control the body's use of fats, proteins, and carbohydrates
- Suppress inflammation
- Support the immune system

Cortisol

Cortisol is a critical "coping hormone." It enables the body to handle both emotional and physical stress. When your body senses a sudden stressful or threatening event, cortisol levels rise quickly. Cortisol has many important roles:

- Maintains emotional stability
- Maintains resistance to stress
- Improves blood volume and blood pressure

- Counters inflammation and allergies
- Increases blood sugar
- Shifts metabolism to utilize sugars

Cortisol is produced and stored while we sleep and so is at its highest level by morning. Throughout the day, levels drop and are at their lowest by midnight. Levels are restored while we are in REM (rapid eye movement) phase sleep around 2:00 to 3:00 in the morning. Interrupted sleep, commonly experienced by women in menopause or during stress, significantly interferes with normal cortisol production.

When you experience stress, cortisol levels quickly rise, shifting you into a "fight-or-flight" mode. Cortisol orchestrates the other hormones so that you can react quickly by raising your heart rate and blood pressure, increasing your muscle strength, and speeding up your reaction time.

If your stress becomes prolonged, excessive amounts of cortisol are released. Constant excessive cortisol release causes high blood pressure, heart disease, bone thinning, weight gain, insomnia, muscle loss, muscle weakness, and abnormal increases in appetite.

Over time it becomes difficult for the adrenals to keep up with the amount of hormones needed to manage chronic stress. Cortisol levels then start to fall below normal. This state of hormone deficiency is called adrenal fatigue. Once you reach this level of adrenal depletion, even antidepressant medications don't work as well. This makes chronic depression more difficult to treat. Chronic fatigue, fibromyalgia, and chronic depression are all characterized by low adrenal activity. Adrenal fatigue puts you at significant risk for developing heart attacks, strokes, and even cancers. This explains why you hear that chronic stress can make you sick.

Adrenal fatigue causes the following symptoms:

- Excessive tiredness
- Muscle weakness
- Mental depression

- Nervousness
- Irritability
- Anxiety
- Inability to concentrate
- Moments of confusion
- Feelings of frustration
- Light-headedness
- Insomnia
- Cravings for sweets and/or salts
- Chronic headaches
- Pain and spasms in the muscles of the upper back/neck/shoulder
- Hypoglycemia (low blood sugar spells)
- Excessive hunger
- Alternating diarrhea and constipation
- Irritable bowel
- Poor resistance to infections
- Heart palpitations
- Dry and thin skin
- Low body temperature
- Unexplained hair loss
- Difficulty building muscle
- Weight-control problems
- Tendency toward inflammation
- Increased susceptibility to cancer
- Increased susceptibility to autoimmune diseases

Measuring and Supporting Cortisol

Janice H.'s experience coping with stress demonstrates the importance of determining whether your cortisol levels are too high or too low. The treatment for each condition is entirely different. Janice ordered a product from a television ad that promised to help her lose weight by lowering her cortisol level. She took it for two months without losing a pound. During that time, her doctor not only had to increase her antidepressant medication to help her manage her mood but also had to add another medication. Janice decided that changing her mood with more medication wasn't worth it, and she quit taking the cortisol-lowering product. When she finally came to see us for weight loss three months later, we measured her baseline cortisol levels. She was surprised to see that her levels were actually quite low. The product she had taken was intended to lower high cortisol levels. She didn't realize that she was blindly lowering her low cortisol levels even further, which accounted for her lack of weight loss and increasing mood and energy problems.

We had her use adrenal glandular supplements to help increase her cortisol. Her energy and mood markedly improved, and she was finally able to start losing weight.

Janice's experience underscores the importance of measuring your baseline cortisol levels to determine whether they are too high or too low. Measurement can be done through saliva or blood testing. If your levels are too high, you can use the supplement phosphorylated serine 90 to 200 milligrams each morning, at least fifteen minutes before eating. Using phosphorylated serine for three to six months will help lower chronically elevated cortisol levels.

If your cortisol levels are too low, use adrenal glandular extract supplements. They are available at many health product stores.

DHEA

Dehydroepiandrosterone (DHEA) is another important hormone secreted by the adrenal glands located above the kidneys. DHEA promotes a positive anabolic (protein-building) state for the body. It lowers the risk of heart attacks and strokes by improving fat metabolism. DHEA stimulates the immune system, restores sexual vitality, improves mood, lowers cholesterol, and reduces body fat. Recent studies point to DHEA as an important antistress hormone. It can reverse the effects of stress on the immune system.

DHEA is similar in structure to testosterone, estrogen, and progesterone. Under various conditions, DHEA can convert to any one of these sex hormones.

DHEA levels normally decrease as we age. Some report that in normal aging humans, DHEA drops so that by age seventy-five, levels are reduced by 80 percent.

Chronic stress overworks the adrenal glands, so DHEA levels are further depleted. This is because precursors for DHEA are rerouted to make cortisol, which is more critical under stress. Low levels of thyroid also decrease amounts of DHEA.

Low DHEA is associated with weight gain, diabetes, depression, immune deficiencies, and low sex drive. Recent studies associate low DHEA levels with increased chances of developing cancer, especially breast cancer.

The metabolism benefits of DHEA include better fat burning and muscle building. These occur because DHEA's functions are similar to those of testosterone, as discussed earlier in this chapter. Like testosterone, DHEA also improves cholesterol ratios.

DHEA strongly influences brain function. Optimal levels improve memory and mental acuity. A study by J. F. Roberts and Eugene Roberts showed that adding DHEA to brain tissue of mice increased their intercellular connectors. The more connections, the quicker the communication and transfer of information occurred among brain cells.

A human study by O. M. Wolkowitz took six elderly men suffering from depression and memory problems and treated them with DHEA. After just one month of treatment, their depression was mostly gone, and they showed dramatic improvement in their collective and detail memory.

In another study, thirteen men and seventeen women, ages forty through seventy, found vast improvements in their mood and energy after treatment with DHEA.

If you have optimal levels of DHEA, you are less likely to develop arteriosclerosis (hardening of the arteries), abnormal cholesterol, Alzheimer's disease, Parkinson's, cancer, and diabetes. Other areas of potential DHEA benefits include improved management of cholesterol, HIV infection, chronic fatigue syndrome, obesity, autoimmune diseases, and herpes.

The following are functions of DHEA:

- Acts as a precursor hormone for testosterone, estrogens, and progesterone
- Reverses immune suppression caused by excess cortisol levels
- Improves resistance to bacteria, viruses, and yeast
- Improves resistance to allergies and cancer
- Prevents osteoporosis
- Improves cholesterol levels
- Increases muscle mass
- Lowers body fat
- Improves energy
- Improves memory
- Improves mood
- Reverses many of the unfavorable effects of cortisol
- Allows quicker recovery from acute stress

DHEA is available without a prescription at most health and nutrition stores. The recommended dose of DHEA is 10 to 25 milligrams daily for women and 25 to 75 milligrams daily for men. Side effects of DHEA include oily skin, acne, itching, or rash. If these occur, decrease your dose or, if severe, discontinue DHEA. Because DHEA is a precursor to all of the sex hormones, including estrogen, there is some concern about using DHEA if you have had a history of estrogen-dependent tumors, such as breast or uterine cancer. If you have a concern about DHEA, consult your physician before using it.

Adrenal Hormones and Serotonin

In stress-prone individuals, a diet high in carbohydrates and low in protein improves depression. One study measured a 42 percent increase in serotonin and a significant lowering of cortisol in a dietary-treated group of stressed test subjects. Researchers concluded, "Stress responses can be improved with the addition of the serotonin-boosting diet recommendations."

Another study showed that subjects under stressful situations were better able to cope while on a high-carbohydrate/low-protein diet as compared to those on a low-carbohydrate/high-protein diet.

Insulin

Insulin is secreted from the pancreas gland and is critical for glucose (sugar) transport to every cell for fuel. If insulin levels are too low or too high, the functions of the cells are greatly impaired. Hyperinsulinemia (too high insulin) contributes to a metabolic syndrome called insulin-resistance syndrome (IRS). Up to 75 percent of American adults have this hormone condition. IRS worsens with age and often results in high blood pressure, abnormal cholesterol and/or triglycerides, obesity, gout, heart disease, stroke, and diabetes. We now recognize that insulin resistance causes the common condition called polycystic ovarian syndrome (PCOS). Because insulin resistance is such an important factor in dieting, we'll discuss the role of insulin more completely in the next chapter.

Main Points in Chapter 5

- Hormones are chemical messengers that are secreted into the blood from glands and affect how well neurotransmitters do their jobs.
- Estrogen, progesterone, testosterone, cortisol, thyroid, and insulin are the main hormones that affect your mood, energy, and appetite and affect how well neurotransmitters do their jobs.
- Women are more susceptible to serotonin changes because of their cyclic hormone changes.
- Testosterone is needed by both men and women to promote metabolism.

- Abnormally high or low stress hormone levels affect the neurotransmitters that control mood, energy, and appetite.
- Postmenopausal women are especially prone to hormone and neurotransmitter deficiencies.
- Hormone levels can be measured and should be maintained at their middle to upper ranges of normal.

6

Insulin Resistance and Serotonin

Insulin is a hormone secreted by the pancreas, a gland located behind the stomach that controls blood sugar. Carbohydrates are broken down during digestion to the simplest sugar, glucose. Insulin regulates how much glucose stays in the blood and how much goes into the cells. If insulin levels are too high or too low, blood sugar levels shift erratically. High blood sugar levels (*hyperglycemia*) lead to diabetes. Low blood sugar (*hypoglycemia*) causes muscle weakness, headaches, sweating, tremors, and mental confusion. The brain is especially sensitive to sudden drops in glucose. If hypoglycemia is severe, seizures and even death can occur.

Insulin Resistance

Many people develop a condition where insulin is blocked from carrying glucose into the cells. We say that the cells have become "insulin resistant." This occurs mainly in the liver, muscle, and fat cells. The pancreas responds by producing more and more insulin to overcome this resistance. Abnormally high insulin levels, hyperinsulinemia, lead to abdominal weight gain, problems with cholesterol and triglycerides, fatty liver, high blood pressure, gout, and polycystic ovaries. As insulin resistance worsens, the pancreas cannot keep up the demand. Blood glucose levels creep up, and diabetes develops.

At least 75 percent of overweight Americans have some degree of insulin resistance. As you become more overweight, insulin resistance worsens. By the same token, the more weight you lose, the less insulin resistant you become.

Insulin Resistance and Fat Cells

In addition to being a carbohydrate or sugar problem, insulin resistance is also a fat-metabolizing problem. Stored excess fat (adipose tissue) becomes less responsive to insulin. Extra calories from food are stored in fat as fatty acids. Even though fat can store fatty acids indefinitely, some spill over into the liver and muscles. When fatty acids or their by-products accumulate in the muscle or liver, they produce a toxic chemical called *ceramide*, which blocks insulin's signal. Ceramide also kills off insulin-producing cells in the pancreas, which triggers still more insulin resistance.

During early stages of insulin resistance, your body compensates by producing large amounts of insulin. Over time, ceramide increases and limits the amount of insulin the pancreas can make. "That's why virtually all overweight people are insulin resistant," says Yale University researcher Gerald Shulman.

Saturated fats, usually from animal fat, turn into ceramide. Not all fats are a problem, though. The monounsaturated fats found in olive oil and the polyunsaturated fats in canola oil do not turn into ceramide. This is one more reason why diets high in animal fats are less healthy than those high in unsaturated vegetable fats. The types of dietary fats found to be the most beneficial are the omega-3 fats. These oils are found in fish, flaxseed, and borage seed. In Chapter 8, we discuss the recommended daily amounts of omega-3 fats.

The Insulin-Resistance Syndrome (IRS)

Insulin resistance leads to a cluster of health conditions that increase your risk of heart attacks, strokes, and diabetes. This set of symptoms is known as the insulin-resistance syndrome or metabolic syndrome.

You have this syndrome if you have *any three* of the following conditions:

- Increased weight gain around your abdomen with a waist measurement of thirty-five inches or more for women and forty inches or more for men
- Triglycerides higher than 150 milligrams/deciliter
- HDL ("good") cholesterol below 50 milligrams/deciliter for women and below 40 milligrams/deciliter for men
- Blood pressure of 130/85 millimeters of mercury or higher
- High fasting blood glucose level of 110 milligrams/deciliter or higher

Insulin resistance affects more than half of America's adults and children. Heredity predisposes many groups of people to this condition. Eating excess amounts of sugary, overly refined foods and saturated fats intensifies the problem. Combining these with the lack of sufficient exercise makes the insulin-resistance syndrome the worst health epidemic in the United States today. In 2001 the National Institutes of Health issued an urgent plea to physicians to screen all of their patients. "The metabolic syndrome has emerged as being as strong a contributor to early heart disease as cigarette smoking. In addition, the insulin resistance that goes along with the syndrome is one of the underlying causes of type 2 diabetes."

Type 2 diabetes increases your chances of heart attack, stroke, kidney failure, blindness, vascular injury, and nerve damage. Health advisers warn that if we do not make drastic lifestyle changes soon, one out of every two American adults and children will develop type 2 diabetes over the next twenty years. The average life span will shorten—by as much as twenty years. Instead of living to the average age of eighty-four, most Americans will die in their midsixties from complications of diabetes. Insurance rates will increase drastically as more demands are made on our health care system.

Insulin resistance and prediabetes usually have no symptoms. You may have one or both conditions for several years without noticing anything. If you have a severe form of insulin resistance, you may get dark patches of skin, usually on the back of your neck. Sometimes people get a dark ring around their neck. Other possible sites for these dark patches include elbows, knees, knuckles, and armpits. This condition is called *acanthosis nigricans*. Another skin phenomenon associated with insulin resistance is the presence of skin tags. These are small, benign, fleshy flaps of skin that sprout on your neck, under your breasts and armpits, on your inner thighs, and, often, on your eyelids. Though often dismissed as a cosmetic nuisance by many doctors, skin tags have been identified as a sign of prediabetes.

You can determine whether you have insulin resistance by completing the following self-test.

Are You at Risk for Insulin Resistance?

This questionnaire will help you identify your risks for insulin resistance and its health complications. It is based on the 2001 National Institutes of Health guidelines for screening for insulin-resistance syndrome, also known as metabolic syndrome.

DIRECTIONS: For each YES answer, circle the assigned number of points. Total all of your points in all three sections to find your final **Insulin-Resistance Risk Score**.

SECTION A: Your Family History

Has anyone in your close family (parents, siblings, grandparents, aunts, uncles) had:

10   Type 2 diabetes or adult-onset diabetes?
10   Heart attack?
10   Stroke?
10   Hardening of the arteries (atherosclerosis)?
10   High blood pressure?
10   Gout?
10   Native American, Latin-American, Asian, or African-American descent?
10   Significant overweight problems (more than fifty pounds overweight)?
8   Moderate overweight problems (thirty to fifty pounds over-weight)?
2   Blood clots in their legs or lungs?
2   Breast, uterine, or ovarian cancer?
1   Osteoarthritis?

TOTAL Points in Section A: _____

SECTION B: Your Nutritional Factors

Do you:

8   Have a sedentary lifestyle and do little or no exercise?
8   Find you cannot lose weight even on a low-fat diet?
10   Have to eat frequently, "graze," or nibble all day to keep up your energy?
8   Find that you *initially* feel better right after eating carbohydrates?
10   Notice that you get extremely tired within an hour after eating sugary or starchy foods?
6   Use caffeine to pep up your energy?
10   Get up in the middle of the night to eat (especially carbohydrates)?

20 Have shakiness, irritability, or problems thinking that go away when you eat?

10 Actually feel better when you don't eat?

TOTAL Points in Section B: _____

SECTION C: Your Health Profile

Do you:

190 Have type 2 diabetes or borderline diabetes?

10 Gain weight around your waist (apple shaped)?

5 Have a BMI (body mass index) between 25 and 27? (See Table 6.1.)

8 Have a BMI between 28 and 30? (See Table 6.1.)

60 Have a BMI greater than 30? (See Table 6.1.)

10 Have (or have you ever had) high blood pressure?

20 Have (or have you ever had) abnormal cholesterol levels?

20 Have (or have you ever had) high triglyceride levels?

20 Have a history of gout?

20 Have fleshy "skin tags" on your neck, eyelids, underarms, or inner thighs or under your breasts?

20 Ever have an abnormal glucose-tolerance test or feel poorly during the test?

20 Have a problem with low blood sugar symptoms?

5 Have a problem with poor circulation of your feet or hands?

5 Have (or have you ever had) a blood clot in your legs or lungs?

4 Have osteoarthritis (common arthritis of aging)?

4 Smoke more than ten cigarettes a day?

20 Have extreme fatigue after eating, especially in the afternoon or evening?

Are you:

5 Between forty-five and sixty years of age?

10 Older than sixty years?

The following apply only to women:

Do you:

20 Have a history of gestational diabetes during any pregnancy?

20 Have a history of having a baby that weighed more than nine pounds?

10 Have a history of toxemia or preeclampsia during any pregnancy?

8 Have a history of high blood pressure during any pregnancy?

20 Have (or have you had a history of) polycystic ovarian syndrome (PCOS)?

TOTAL Points in Section C: _____

Add up your points from all three sections to get your total insulin-resistance score:

Section A _____ **+ Section B** _____ **+ Section C** _____ **=**

TOTAL Insulin-Resistance Risk Score of _____

Total Score Interpretation

60–90: Stage I. This *early stage* suggests that you may be at risk for developing insulin resistance.

91–120: Stage II. You have an *above average risk* of developing insulin resistance.

121–150: Stage III. You are *showing definite signs* of insulin resistance.

151–180: Stage IV. You have insulin resistance and have *significant conditions associated with insulin-resistance syndrome.*

More than 180: Stage V. This score warns you that you have *severe insulin resistance.* Type 2 diabetes, heart attack, and stroke are definite health risks for you. You should manage your insulin-resistance condition aggressively to avoid these complications.

From the National Institutes of Health, 2001. National Heart, Lung, and Blood Institute: National Cholesterol Education Program.

TABLE 6.1   What's My Body Mass Index?

Height	Body weight in pounds																
4'10"	91	96	100	105	110	115	119	124	129	134	138	143	148	153	158	162	167
4'11"	94	99	104	109	114	119	124	128	133	138	143	148	153	158	163	168	173
5'0"	97	102	107	112	118	123	128	133	138	143	148	153	158	163	168	174	179
5'1"	100	106	111	116	122	127	132	137	143	148	153	158	164	169	174	180	185
5'2"	104	109	115	120	126	131	136	142	147	153	158	164	169	175	180	186	191
5'3"	107	113	118	124	130	135	141	146	152	158	163	169	175	180	186	191	197
5'4"	110	116	122	128	134	140	145	151	157	163	169	174	180	186	192	197	204
5'5"	114	120	126	132	138	144	150	156	162	168	174	180	186	192	198	204	210
5'6"	118	124	130	136	142	148	155	161	167	173	179	186	192	198	204	210	216
5'7"	121	127	134	140	146	153	159	166	172	178	185	191	198	204	211	217	223
5'8"	125	131	138	144	151	158	164	171	177	184	190	197	203	210	216	223	230
5'9"	128	135	142	149	155	162	169	176	182	189	196	203	209	216	223	230	236
5'10"	132	139	146	153	160	167	174	181	188	195	202	207	216	222	229	236	243
5'11"	136	143	150	157	165	172	179	186	193	200	208	215	222	229	236	243	250
6'0"	140	147	154	162	169	177	184	191	199	206	213	221	228	235	242	250	258
6'1"	144	151	159	166	174	182	189	197	204	212	219	227	235	242	250	257	265
6'2"	148	155	163	171	179	186	194	202	210	218	225	233	241	249	256	264	272
6'3"	152	160	168	176	184	192	200	208	216	224	232	240	248	256	264	272	279
6'4"	156	164	172	180	189	197	205	213	221	230	238	246	254	263	271	279	287
BMI	19	20	21	22	23	24	25	26	27	28	29	30	31	32	33	34	35

Healthy Weight   Overweight   Obese

Detecting and Preventing Type 2 Diabetes

You don't get type 2 diabetes overnight. It *always* starts as insulin resistance and takes about ten years to develop into diabetes. This means that type 2 diabetes is *preventable* when you identify and tend to it early.

Blood glucose levels that are higher than normal but not yet in the diabetic range are considered borderline or prediabetes.

Insulin resistance and prediabetes can be detected with one of the following blood tests:

- A **fasting glucose** test measures blood glucose after you have gone without eating for more than six hours. This test is usually done first thing in the morning. Normal fasting glucose levels range from 65 to 99 milligrams/deciliter. A fasting glucose level between 99 and 120 milligrams/deciliter means you have prediabetes. Even at lower glucose levels you can predict the likelihood of developing diabetes. Look for an upward trend from your previous glucose levels. Even though your levels may not yet be in a prediabetic range, a rising pattern should alert you. Fasting glucose levels above 100 milligrams/deciliter but less than 120 milligrams/deciliter should concern you. Because diabetes is still preventable at this stage, making immediate changes in your diet and activity will help you avoid diabetes.
- **Fasting insulin** is another test for insulin resistance. It measures your blood insulin after an overnight fast. Even though you may have normal glucose levels, you can still have a high insulin level. Normal insulin levels should be low in the morning because you have not yet eaten. Levels greater than 10 mIU/deciliter are suspicious for insulin resistance. A level greater than 23 mIU/deciliter is called hyperinsulinemia and diagnoses insulin resistance.

Most people with insulin resistance or prediabetes go on to develop type 2 diabetes within ten years. Recent studies show that losing just 5 to 7 percent of your body weight reduces chances of developing diabetes by 58 percent. This means that for someone weighing two hundred pounds, losing just ten to fifteen pounds can make the difference in getting or preventing diabetes.

In our previous book, *The Insulin-Resistance Diet* (McGraw-Hill, 2001), we introduced a method of regulating insulin by linking and balancing foods. By combining specific portions of high-carbohydrate foods with high-protein foods, insulin can be controlled. Our Link-and-Balance Method leads to successful weight loss without eliminating any one particular food group. Our Feel-Good Diet plan modifies this method to control insulin while also supporting neurotransmitter production. This method is provided in Chapter 7.

Calcium for Weight Loss and for Reducing Insulin Resistance

Several animal studies have shown that increased calcium intake in mice resulted in decreased fat storage, increased metabolism, and more fat breakdown. Human studies also find a strong connection between calcium intake and weight. Women with the highest calcium intake had the lowest body fat. In fact, one study showed that women who ate the least calcium were twice as likely to be overweight. Another study showed that women who ate a higher ratio of calcium to calories had the largest decrease in body fat during exercise, no matter what kind of exercise the subjects did.

Researchers Robert Heaney and K. Michael Davies conclude that every 300 milligrams of calcium consumed on a daily basis results in six pounds less body weight in women. One cup of milk contains about 300 milligrams. Children showed two pounds less body fat per every 300 milligrams of calcium in their diet.

Men with low calcium intake also tended to be overweight. Men who consume adequate calcium are less likely to be overweight, but additional calcium does not seem to decrease weight in men, as it does in women and children. In another study on both men and women, more calcium intake was associated with higher rates of fat burning, even during sleep.

In both animals and humans, calcium intake from dairy sources shows better results than when calcium is from supplements. In humans, dairy calcium decreased fat the most in the abdominal area. Abdominal fat is highly associated with insulin resistance.

For those of you who are concerned about insulin resistance, dairy calcium seems to help this health issue as well. In a ten-year study on more than three thousand men and women, researchers found that greater dairy consumption resulted in decreased occurrence of insulin-resistance syndrome. In fact, in those subjects with the highest dairy intake, the study found 72 percent less incidence of IRS after ten years. Another study looked at more than ten thousand women over forty-five years old who participated in the Women's Health Initiative Study. The researchers found that the women who had higher intakes of dietary calcium (from dairy) and supplemental calcium had significantly less insulin resistance. These findings show that adequate calcium can help reduce your risk of diabetes and heart disease, two very deadly diseases.

If you have lost weight and want to keep it off, keep that calcium going. The National Weight Control Registry monitors subjects who have lost at least thirty pounds and have kept it off for at least one year. They compile data on participants, including calcium intake. Their data show that the best weight maintainers consume more calcium than the average American.

So, how much calcium should you include each day? More studies are being done to determine the optimal amount, but at this time we know these things:

- Consuming less than the recommended amount of calcium for your age and gender seems to result in more weight and other health issues. See Table 6.2 to find your recommended amount of daily calcium.
- Consuming more than 2,500 milligrams per day may be bad for your health because of kidney problems including kidney stones.

TABLE 6.2 Recommended Minimum Amounts of Daily Calcium

AGE	ADEQUATE INTAKE PER DAY
0–6 months	210 milligrams
6–12 months	270 milligrams
1–3 years	500 milligrams
4–8 years	800 milligrams
9–18 years	1,300 milligrams
19–50 years	1,000 milligrams
51 years and up	1,200 milligrams

- Adequate calcium can be achieved by consuming four servings of dairy foods per day. See Table 6.3 for food sources of calcium.

If you need to take supplements to get enough calcium, it is best to take no more than 500 milligrams at a time and to be sure to get adequate vitamin D either in your calcium or your daily multiple. Take calcium with dairy foods to enhance absorption. Try not to take it at the same time as a multivitamin/mineral supplement because some minerals bind to the calcium and decrease absorption. Oxalic acid, found in leafy greens, and phytic acid from wheat bran and beans also bind calcium and result in less absorption.

It is time to think of calcium in a whole new way. It's not just good for your bones. It may save your life.

For more information on calcium and weight loss, go to national dairycouncil.org/healthyweight/science.asp.

Stress and Insulin Resistance

Stress increases insulin resistance, ultimately promoting obesity, abnormal lipids, and hypertension. In Chapter 5, we reviewed the hormone responses to stress. This eventually results in increased cortisol levels. High cortisol increases the production of insulin. Both excess cortisol and excess insulin signal your body to make more fatty

TABLE 6.3 Food Sources of Calcium

FOOD	SERVING SIZE	CALCIUM CONTENT
Yogurt, plain or with fruit, low-fat or nonfat	1 cup	400–450 milligrams
Milk, nonfat, low-fat, or whole	1 cup	90–300 milligrams
Cheese, cheddar, Swiss, American, or mozzarella	1 ounce	152–200 milligrams
Cheese, Parmesan or Romano	1 ounce	318 milligrams
Cheese, cottage	¼ cup	38 milligrams
Buttermilk or chocolate milk	1 cup	285 milligrams
Frozen yogurt	½ cup	85–105 milligrams
Soy milk (with added calcium)	1 cup	80–200 milligrams
Tofu (made with calcium sulfate)	½ cup	258 milligrams
Calcium-fortified orange juice	½ cup	175–300 milligrams
Salmon, canned (with bones)	3 ounces	180 milligrams
Sardines, canned (with bones)	3 ounces	203–260 milligrams
Kale or bok choy, cooked	½ cup	90 milligrams
Turnip greens	½ cup	125 milligrams
Collard greens	½ cup	177 milligrams
Broccoli	½ cup	45 milligrams
Ready-to-eat cereals, calcium fortified	Varies	100–1,000 milligrams

acids, which results in more fat. Research has shown that increased adipose (fat) tissue gets in the way of insulin absorption, increasing insulin resistance.

To make matters worse, insulin resistance is associated with lowering levels of serotonin. Because serotonin is our major "coping" neurotransmitter, having less of it makes the effects of stress more severe, further increasing cortisol. E. Epel found that women who had a high cortisol response to stress ate more calories and sweeter calories when put under stress than women who handled the same stress with less reaction. So you can see how constantly reacting to stress can result in a negative spiral of increasing insulin resistance and decreasing serotonin. By learning and practicing methods to reduce your "stress response," you can reverse this negative spiral.

The Insulin-Serotonin Dilemma

In our previous book, *The Insulin-Resistance Diet*, we discussed dietary control of insulin to treat the condition called insulin resistance. High insulin levels can lead to weight gain, high blood pressure, abnormal cholesterol, high triglycerides, diabetes, heart attacks, and strokes. High-carbohydrate foods abnormally raise insulin, making insulin resistance worse. Protein, on the other hand, improves insulin resistance.

Other diets such as Atkins and South Beach also help manage insulin resistance. They lower insulin by severely restricting the amount of high-carbohydrate foods that you are allowed to eat. The South Beach Diet limits simple-carbohydrate foods more than complex ones, but the net result is still a low-carbohydrate/high-protein diet. What these low-carbohydrate diets don't consider, however, is the damaging effect they have on the production of neurotransmitters, especially serotonin.

The neurotransmitters that regulate mood, energy, appetite, and sex drive are made from amino acids, the building blocks of protein.

The amounts and kinds of amino acids contained in certain foods determine which neurotransmitters are made and which ones are blocked.

Tryptophan is the amino acid necessary for making serotonin. The amino acids tyrosine and phenylalanine are the building blocks for dopamine and norepinephrine. Chapter 3 reviews the pathways for making these.

Research by J. D. Fernstrom found that when you eat protein, not all of its amino acids reach the brain at the same time. They compete for absorption into the brain. The most abundant amino acids win and are absorbed first. If more tyrosine and phenylalanine are present, neurons make more of the catecholamines, dopamine and norepinephrine. When tryptophan dominates, more of the calming neurotransmitter serotonin is produced.

High-protein foods always have more tyrosine in them than tryptophan. In fact, of the twenty-two amino acids found in protein, tryptophan is the least abundant. After eating a meal high in protein, the amino acids absorb into the blood circulation. Because it is so abundant, tyrosine absorbs first into the brain. Tyrosine favors production of dopamine and norepinephrine but decreases production of serotonin.

A high-protein diet severely restricts the production of serotonin. Tryptophan, necessary for serotonin production, is blocked from entering the brain because of the presence of other more abundant amino acids, namely tyrosine and phenylalanine. This blocking effect lasts for up to three hours after eating a high-protein meal. Even a meal containing as little as 10 percent of its total calories from protein will result in lowering of serotonin levels.

Likewise, a meal containing carbohydrates and no protein markedly increases the absorption of tryptophan into the brain. A high-carbohydrate meal produces more serotonin and less dopamine.

The way carbohydrates increase serotonin is fascinating, especially because there is no tryptophan in high-carbohydrate foods.

Here's where the hormone insulin enters the picture. After we eat carbohydrates, blood glucose (blood sugar) levels normally rise. Insulin is immediately released to readjust blood glucose levels. Insulin takes extra glucose to the muscles for energy use. Insulin also attracts muscle-building amino acids toward the muscles. In this way, insulin performs a double duty for muscles—delivering glucose for energy and amino acids for building and repair. With most of the amino acids now out of circulation, tryptophan can now easily sneak into the brain to produce serotonin. Interestingly, any carbohydrate that elicits insulin secretion can produce a rise in serotonin. This response is independent of the food's sweetness, as long as the food in which the carbohydrate comes from (e.g., pasta) does not contain more than 12 percent protein.

This helps to explain why people with low serotonin often crave high-carbohydrate foods. The more carbohydrates you eat, the more serotonin you make and the better you feel.

Men have one-third more serotonin than women do. This is because they have more muscle than women. Men divert more amino acids to their muscles for building and repair. This clears the way for a lot more tryptophan to enter the brain for serotonin production. In their attempt to keep up with producing enough serotonin, it's no wonder that women usually crave more carbohydrates than men do.

There has been a lot of recent research linking serotonin deficiencies in women with low-carbohydrate diets. Here is a summary of the startling conclusions.

- In women only, serotonin levels drop significantly after three weeks of being on any type of diet.
- Diets that severely restrict carbohydrates result in even further lowering of serotonin levels. Dr. Judith Wurtman of MIT found that women on high-protein diets with very low carbohydrate intake are at high risk for developing binge disorders, depression, seasonal affective disorder (SAD), and severe premenstrual

syndrome (PMS) or premenstrual dysphoric disorder (PMDD) symptoms.

Now the insulin-serotonin dilemma should be clearer to you (see Figure 6.1).

- **The dilemma:** Diets that lower insulin resistance (high protein/ low carbohydrate) also lower serotonin. So . . . how do you limit carbohydrates enough to control insulin resistance and yet eat enough of them to make serotonin?
- **The solution:** In *The Insulin-Resistance Diet*, we presented the Link-and-Balance Method for controlling the body's insulin response to carbohydrates. It works by linking carbohydrates with a balanced amount of protein during the same meal. Now, our Feel-Good Diet plan shows you a method of controlling insulin while at the same time increasing serotonin production.

FIGURE 6.1 Insulin-Serotonin Dilemma

Controlling insulin requires limiting carbohydrates.

But carbohydrates are needed to make more serotonin.

A diet too low in carbohydrates and too high in protein prevents serotonin production.

In Chapters 10, 11, 12, and 13 we show you the four ways to do this:

- Improving your neurotransmitters with food
- Using supplements to further increase and balance your neuro-transmitters
- Improving your metabolism and energy
- Increasing neurotransmitters with exercise and other activities

Main Points in Chapter 6

- Excess insulin causes weight gain, especially around your waist.
- Insulin-resistance syndrome is a cluster of medical conditions that include weight gain, abnormal cholesterol, high blood pressure, high triglyceride levels, and glucose intolerance.
- The more overweight you are, the more insulin resistant you become.
- Insulin resistance is associated with low levels of serotonin.
- High-protein foods improve insulin resistance but lower serotonin levels.
- High-carbohydrate foods raise serotonin levels but worsen insulin resistance.
- Women on high-protein diets are more susceptible to serotonin problems.
- The Feel-Good Diet plan combines proteins and carbohydrates in ways that control insulin resistance while improving serotonin.

PART II

The Feel-Good Weight-Loss Program

7

Feeling Good with Food

In our book *The Insulin-Resistance Diet*, we focused primarily on controlling insulin. This has been very successful in treating high blood pressure, high cholesterol, prediabetes, as well as weight. All of these issues are related to insulin resistance. As we discussed in Chapter 6, the dilemma is that controlling insulin can also decrease the brain's ability to make serotonin.

Now that you know about the importance of neurotransmitters such as serotonin and the serotonin-insulin dilemma, what can you do about it? How do you get enough carbohydrates to help make serotonin without creating conditions that worsen insulin resistance?

In our recent research and daily practice with women at our Wellness Workshop, we found the best way is to combine two eating methods—one that controls insulin and another that increases serotonin—to get the best of both worlds. Lowering insulin improves your weight loss, corrects high blood pressure, controls blood sugar, and lowers your cholesterol and triglycerides. Raising serotonin improves your mood and energy and controls your appetite and cravings. The first eating method, Plan I, is a modified version of our successful Link-and-Balance Method used to control insulin. Once we explain the basics, we will show you how we improved it to increase your serotonin.

Most of us can effectively control our insulin levels while boosting our serotonin with the snacks presented in Plan I. But if you are severely insulin resistant (see Chapter 6) or if you get dizzy or very tired after having one of the serotonin-boosting snacks, then you will do better on Plan II. Plan II uses serotonin-boosting supplements and is presented in Chapters 10 and 13.

Controlling Insulin Resistance

We have simplified our insulin-controlling Link-and-Balance Method by dividing foods into four groups according to how much they stimulate or "spike" insulin. The higher the spike, the more they stimulate insulin. Foods are labeled high-insulin-spiking foods, low-insulin-spiking foods, and insulin-neutral foods. The fourth group, nonlinking fresh fruits, includes certain fruits that affect insulin differently from many of the other fruits. Our patients like this way of categorizing foods because it eliminates the burden of counting calories, keeping food diaries, tracking "points," comparing charts, or referring to glycemic index tables.

High-Insulin-Spiking Food Group

High-insulin-spiking foods are high in carbohydrates and very low in protein. The more refined and processed the carbohydrates are, the higher they spike your insulin. They include the following:

- Any foods with added sugar, especially high-fructose corn syrup
- All grains

- Most fruits, *except fresh forms* of apples, apricots, cherries, peaches, plums, pears, nectarines, grapefruit, lemons, and limes (These exceptions fit into the special nonlinking fruit group and are discussed later.)
- Corn
- Potatoes—all kinds

High-Fructose Corn Syrup: It's Supersweet, Supercheap, and . . . Super Deadly

The heart-healthy campaigns of the 1970s that encouraged Americans to eat low-fat foods were considered successful in that they raised our awareness about cholesterol. By weight-loss standards, however, they failed miserably. Despite eating less fat in foods, Americans kept getting fatter.

It seems that when food manufacturers took out all the fat, they needed to add something back. They made food sweeter so it would taste better and keep selling. They started using an inexpensive corn syrup known as high-fructose modified corn syrup (also called HFCS).

Since the 1970s, food manufacturers have replaced most other sweeteners, including sugar, with this genetically modified supersweet corn syrup. Worse yet, they started adding it to foods that were previously not sweetened.

The U.S. Department of Agriculture food consumption tables show that there has been a 1,000 percent increase of high-fructose corn syrup consumption between 1970 and 1990. This far exceeds the changes in the intake of any other food or food groups. The use of high-fructose corn syrup now represents more than 40 percent of the caloric sweeteners added to foods and beverages. It is the sole caloric sweetener in soft drinks in the United States. Recent research estimates that all Americans two years or older ingest an average of 132 calories from high-fructose corn syrup every day. (This compares to only 80 calories from sweeteners in 1977.) The top 20 percent of consumers of caloric sweeteners ingest 316 calories each day from high-fructose corn syrup in foods. And the result of all this is that by eating an extra 132 calories a day you will gain thirteen extra pounds a year, and eating 316 extra calories a day adds on a whopping thirty-two extra pounds a year.

A 2003 report from the International Obesity Task Force, an affiliate with the World Health Organization, raised concern that high-fructose corn syrup was contributing to the obesity epidemic in the United States. The report questioned whether high-fructose corn syrup might be addictive, citing studies where children preferred processed foods containing high levels of high-fructose corn syrup to the homemade food choices that were made with cane sugar and were less sweet.

In addition to the extra weight you gain from the extra calories, high-fructose corn syrup also causes unique health problems. Our bodies treat fructose in a much different way from how they treat the simple sugar glucose. Immediately after digestion, fructose goes straight to the liver rather than circulating all over the body as glucose does. Once in the liver, fructose is made into fats called triglycerides. Excess fructose raises triglyceride levels, which clog arteries, leading to heart attacks and strokes. Many are aware of how bad excess cholesterol can be, but few realize that high triglycerides may be even worse for your health. A University of Minnesota study fed healthy volunteers a diet containing 17 percent of their total daily calories as fructose for six weeks. (This equals 255 calories of a 1,500-calorie-a-day diet.) This may sound like a lot of calories from fructose, but it is the average amount of fructose eaten by at least twenty-seven million Americans every day. The researchers then fed the volunteers a diet sweetened only with glucose and no fructose. The results were dramatic. The fructose diet produced 32 percent *higher* blood triglyceride levels compared to the glucose diet. Because high triglycerides, obesity, and type 2 diabetes are clearly associated with high-fructose corn syrup, it's no wonder that it is implicated as a major cause of insulin-resistance syndrome. As published in 2005 in the journal

Nutrition & Metabolism, researchers attempting to find solutions for the obesity and diabetes epidemic agree there is an "urgent need for increased public awareness of the risks associated with high fructose consumption and greater efforts should be made to curb the supplementation of package foods with high fructose additives."

Foods containing high-fructose corn syrup stimulate insulin more than any other kind of sugar or sweetener. High-fructose corn syrup changes foods into Superhigh Insulin-Spiking foods. Unfortunately, food manufacturers prefer using high-fructose corn syrup as their sweetener of choice because it is cheap and easily dissolves in all foods. Americans have become addicted to sweetness, and so high-fructose corn syrup appears to be in almost everything. If you look at food labels of most processed foods, you will be shocked to see how often high-fructose corn syrup is added as an ingredient, even in foods that never used to be considered sweet. High-fructose corn syrup is the sweetener most widely used in regular soft drinks, and soda has been recognized as the greatest obesity and diabetic culprit of all time. The rise in diabetes among children over the past ten years has reached epidemic proportions. Because children are the highest consumers of soda, concern has been raised about the health hazards of high-fructose corn syrup. Some states, including Arkansas, Tennessee, Washington, and West Virginia, have even imposed soda taxes to help cover the costs of rising health care needs associated with obesity and diabetes.

Low-Insulin-Spiking Food Group

The low-insulin-spiking foods are mainly high in protein, even though they may also contain some carbohydrates. They include the following:

- All animal proteins such as meat, poultry, and fish
- Eggs
- Dairy foods that have no added sugar

- Legumes and dried beans
- Nuts and seeds

Dairy includes milk, cheese, cottage cheese, and yogurt. Even though dairy foods contain the carbohydrate lactose, their effects on insulin are much different from that of other carbohydrates. However, if sugar is added to a dairy food, it becomes a high-insulin-spiking food. For example, plain milk is a low-insulin spiker, whereas chocolate milk with added sugar is a high-insulin spiker. Legumes, dried beans, and dried peas include soybeans; lentils; garbanzo, kidney, navy, and black beans; and black-eyed and split peas.

Insulin-Neutral Foods

This category includes all other vegetables or plants *not included* in any other group.

These vegetables contain both protein and carbohydrates and are naturally insulin-balanced. They are mostly made up of water and fiber, so you can use them in large quantities if you desire.

Nonlinking Fresh Fruits

Nonlinking fresh fruits is a special group of fruits. In their *fresh form*, they have a weaker effect on insulin than most other fruits. They do not have to be "linked," as do the other fruits. The nonlinking fresh fruits include apples, apricots, cherries, peaches, pears, plums, nectarines, grapefruit, lemons, and limes.

These fruits, however, convert to high-insulin-spiking fruits if they are processed, canned, dried, juiced, or cooked. Under these circumstances, they would then need to be "linked" with a low-insulin-spiking food.

See Table 7.1 for a summary of the food groups. A detailed food index appears at the end of the chapter.

TABLE 7.1 Summary of Link-and-Balance Food Groups

HIGH-INSULIN-SPIKING GROUP	LOW-INSULIN-SPIKING GROUP
Any foods with sugar added	All meats, fish, and poultry
All grains	Eggs
Most fruits (except those listed as nonlinking fresh fruits)	Dairy products (with no added sugar)
Corn	Legumes and dried beans
Potatoes (all kinds)	Nuts and seeds

INSULIN-NEUTRAL GROUP		
All plants not listed in any other group, including tomatoes and avocados		

NONLINKING FRESH FRUITS		
Apples	Pears	Nectarines
Apricots	Plums	Lemons
Cherries	Grapefruit	Limes
Peaches		

The Link-and-Balance Method

The simplest way to manage insulin resistance is to link and balance your meals. *Linking* means eating a low-insulin-spiking food whenever you eat a high-insulin-spiking food. In this way, the insulin peak caused by a high carbohydrate is offset by the lowering effect of a protein-rich food. *Balancing* tells you the portion sizes of food that you need to link with. Linking and balancing allows you to eat carbohydrates while still maintaining fairly normal levels of insulin and balanced blood sugar levels. Foods listed in the insulin-neutral and nonlinking fresh fruit groups can be eaten without linking and balancing.

Even though overall calories make a difference in body weight, you will have greater success with this program if you put the emphasis on controlling your insulin by linking and balancing rather than on counting calories. We have calculated the daily calorie intakes of each of the plans that we present. Our program allows about 1,100 to 1,200 calories for most women and 1,400 to 1,800 calories for most men and very active women.

Know Your Portion Sizes

In addition to knowing which foods to link, it is also important to know their serving sizes so you can balance them properly.

One Serving of a High-Insulin-Spiking Food Equals

- ½ cup of cooked potatoes, corn, rice, pasta, oats, and other grains
- One slice of bread

One Serving of a Low-Insulin-Spiking Food Equals

- One egg
- One ounce of meat, poultry, or fish
- One cup of milk, cottage cheese, or yogurt (no sugar added)
- One slice or one ounce of cheese
- One piece of string cheese
- Two tablespoons of peanut butter or other nut butter
- Three tablespoons of fat-free cream cheese
- ⅓ cup of legumes

Estimating Your Portion Sizes. You can easily estimate food portions by comparing them to the dimensions of your fingers and hand (see Figure 7.1). The length, width, and thickness of two fingers equal about one ounce of meat, fish, poultry, or cheese. The size and thickness of a woman's palm equals four ounces of meat, fish, poultry, or cheese. The size of the palm also approximates a half cup serving of a high-insulin-spiking food such as rice, corn, potatoes, or other grains. The size of a woman's fist approximates one cup of a high-insulin-spiking food.

FIGURE 7.1 Estimating Portion Sizes

2 Fingers = 1 ounce

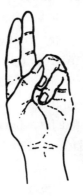

Size of a Woman's Palm = ½ cup or 4 ounces

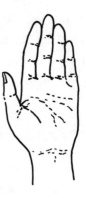

Size of a Woman's Fist = 1 cup

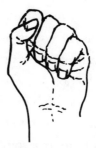

As you link and balance, make all your choices as low in fat content as possible. Even though insulin resistance is mainly about carbohydrate control, overall calories still matter. Fats are "calorie dense" because they contain more than twice as many calories as do carbohydrates and protein. The type of fats you eat are also important. Limit saturated and hydrogenated fats to no more than 10 percent of your total daily calories. This equals fewer than 17 grams a day for women and fewer than 22 grams a day for men. For instance, a lean sirloin steak contains 1 gram of saturated fat per ounce. An ounce of lean ground beef has 2 grams of saturated fat. An ounce of regular ground beef contains 3 grams of saturated fat. One ounce of cheese contains 5 grams of saturated fat. You are eating 13 grams of saturated fat when you have a quarter-pound hamburger with cheese. Saturated and trans fats are listed on the nutrition facts section of food labels.

Healthy fats are known as unsaturated fats. The most important dietary ones for neurotransmitters are the omega-3 and omega-6 fats, which are discussed in detail in Chapter 8.

Serotonin-Boosting Snacks

In Chapter 6, we emphasized that you need to raise insulin in order to increase serotonin. High-insulin-spiking foods raise serotonin. However, if you mainly eat high-insulin-spiking foods, you become more and more insulin resistant. There is also evidence that you become serotonin resistant as well. In other words, the mechanism that usually transports the amino acid tryptophan into the brain for serotonin production stops functioning when it is overworked.

Recall that diets high in protein actually limit the amount of serotonin that your brain can make. Without enough serotonin, you may lose the ability to control your appetite and cravings within just a few weeks of dieting. To help sustain willpower and appetite control, we have instituted serotonin-boosting snacks, which are strategically timed throughout the day. Eating a single serving of a high-insulin-spiking food in the midmorning, afternoon, and evening raises serotonin.

The timing and portion size of your high-insulin-spiking snack is key to making this method work. Research shows that a high-protein meal blocks production of serotonin for three hours. Therefore, it is important to wait at least three hours after having your linked-and-balanced meal to eat your serotonin-boosting snack. Your next linked-and-balanced meal (containing protein) can follow about two hours after your snack. Plan I of the Feel-Good Diet allows you to control your blood sugar and insulin levels throughout the day while intermittently boosting critical serotonin levels with special snacks.

Drinking Super pH Water, as described in Chapter 11, is also helpful for controlling insulin while raising serotonin. This drink acts as a carbo-blocker.

Basics of the Feel-Good Diet Plan I

These daily eating schedules help you make more serotonin while still controlling your insulin resistance. (See Table 7.2.)

1. Choose the one of these daily eating plans that best applies to you:
   - **Plan I-A** works best for most women for weight loss. It approximates 1,100 to 1,200 calories daily.
   - **Plan I-B** works well for most men, women who are exercising several hours a day, or women who are just beginning a muscle-building exercise routine. It contains more protein to build more muscles. Plan B approximates 1,400 to 1,500 calories daily.
   - **Plan I-C** works well for men who exercise several hours daily or who are just beginning a muscle-building routine. It is higher in protein and allows about 1,600 to 1,800 daily calories.
2. Choose from the high- and low-insulin-spiking food lists found at the end of the chapter.
3. Include daily doses of serotonin-supporting cofactor vitamins and minerals. Foods high in calcium are found in Table 6.2. Foods high in magnesium are found in Chapter 11. The best-absorbed minerals are in the aspartate or orotate forms:

TABLE 7.2 Feel-Good Diet Plans At-a-Glance

	BREAKFAST	MORNING SEROTONIN-BOOSTING SNACK	LUNCH	
Plan I-A (weight loss for most women)	Hi – Lo Lo	Hi	Hi – Lo Lo	
Plan I-B (weight loss for very active women and for less-active men)	Hi – Lo Lo	Hi	Hi – Lo × 4	
Plan I-C (weight loss for active men)	Hi Hi – Lo × 4	Hi	Hi – Lo × 4	

Hi = One serving of high-insulin-spiking food   **Lo** = One serving of low-insulin-spiking food

- Calcium—1,000 milligrams as calcium aspartate or calcium oratate
- Magnesium—500 to 1,000 milligrams of magnesium aspartate or magnesium orotate
- Zinc—15 milligrams as elemental zinc
- Time-release vitamin C ascorbate (Ester-C)—500 to 1,000 milligrams
- Time-release vitamin B-50 or B-100 complex

4. Use the following daily schedule, filling in the approximate times of day that work best for you.

One Super pH Water Serving *Before Eating Breakfast*

_____ : _____ A.M. (Write the usual time you get up.)

For Plans I-A, I-B, or I-C, drink one eight-ounce serving of Super pH Water in the morning before you eat or drink anything else. The Super pH Water recipe and dosing recommendations are given in Chapter 11.

AFTERNOON SEROTONIN-BOOSTING SNACK	DINNER	EVENING SEROTONIN-BOOSTING SNACK
Hi	Hi – Lo Lo	Hi
Hi	Hi – Lo × 4	Hi
Hi	Hi – Lo × 4	Hi

Metabolism Goal. Having Super pH Water the first thing in the morning will start your metabolic engine. Super pH Water removes cell acid wastes that have accumulated during the night, corrects cell pH, and allows more oxygen to get into cells. Chapter 11 offers more details on how Super pH Water increases your metabolism.

Hormone Goal. Apple cider vinegar inhibits the enzymes that break down sugars. As a natural carbo-blocker, this lowers the glycemic index of carbohydrates and improves insulin resistance. The total amount of apple cider vinegar recommended is three tablespoons per day. Be sure to dilute the vinegar in water. Avoid drinking concentrated apple cider vinegar and exceeding this recommended amount. Too much vinegar can erode tooth enamel and cause stomach cramps, intestinal upset, and diarrhea. It is best to drink your Super pH Water before each meal.

You may eat your meals any time after drinking the Super pH Water.

Breakfast Meal

At approximately _____ : _____ A.M.

1. Choose one of the following plans:
   - **Plan I-A breakfast:** Eat one serving of a high-insulin-spiking food with two servings of low-insulin-spiking foods.
   - **Plan I-B breakfast:** Eat one serving of a high-insulin-spiking food with two servings of low-insulin-spiking foods.
   - **Plan I-C breakfast:** Eat two servings of high-insulin-spiking foods with four servings of low-insulin-spiking foods.
2. Include foods high in omega-3 fats, or supplement daily with 1,000 milligrams of omega-3 oil.
3. Remember to include at least five servings of insulin-neutral foods daily as desired, at any time of the day.
4. Include two to three servings of fruits each day. Remember that high-insulin-spiking fruits need to be linked whereas nonlinking fresh fruits may be eaten by themselves at any time.
5. Include a daily multivitamin as well as the vitamins and minerals necessary for neurotransmitter production covered earlier in this chapter.

The food combination of your morning meal achieves the following:

Nutritional Goal. The morning meal supplies your body with the carbohydrates necessary to rev up your brain and energy engines for the day. The protein helps begin building and repairing your body.

Dietary fats, especially omega-3s, are necessary for brain and nerve cells as well as for hormone production.

The current recommendation for daily fluid intake is six to eight eight-ounce servings of water or noncaffeinated beverages a day with an additional eight-ounce serving for every twenty-five pounds you are overweight.

Fruits and vegetables in the insulin-neutral food group are high in fiber and supply valuable vitamins, minerals, and antioxidants.

Metabolism Goal. Optimal amounts of glucose are provided for cell functions, yet excessive sugar burning is avoided. Sugar burning produces cell acid wastes, which slow down metabolism.

Hormone Goal. Insulin is controlled by linking and balancing high-insulin-spiking foods with low-insulin-spiking foods. This balance helps control the stress hormones, cortisol and DHEA. Chapter 5 gives details about how hormones affect your neurotransmitters and metabolism.

Neurotransmitter Goal. The amino acids contained in low-insulin-spiking foods provide the building blocks for making neurotransmitters, especially serotonin and dopamine. Serotonin needs tryptophan, and dopamine requires tyrosine. These are explained in Chapter 3.

Midmorning Serotonin-Boosting Snack
At approximately _____ :_____ A.M.

Eat this snack *at least three hours* after finishing breakfast.

For all plans, choose one serving from the high-insulin-spiking food list. It can take one to four hours for the brain to make serotonin from high-carbohydrate foods. Because of this time lag, it is important to start producing serotonin in the morning. This way you avoid falling short of serotonin by the later part of the day, as it is difficult to catch up on once depleted.

It is a tricky balance between trying to regulate your insulin and making enough serotonin. Limit your serotonin-boosting snack to only one serving in order to avoid exaggerating your insulin response.

In the special case of making serotonin, it is important to wait *three hours* after eating a linked-and-balanced meal before having your serotonin-boosting snack. The meals are higher in protein compared to carbohydrates and so prevent serotonin production. Also, avoid combining your serotonin-boosting snack with a low-insulin-spiking food. This is because low-insulin-spiking foods contain too much (more than 12 percent) protein and block serotonin production.

Lunch Meal

At approximately _____ : _____ **P.M.**

Before eating your lunch, drink another eight ounces of Super pH Water. Drinking the Super pH Water before each meal improves your insulin resistance. It also neutralizes acid wastes that continue to form in cells throughout the day.

1. Choose one of the following plans:
   - **Plan I-A lunch meal:** Eat one serving of a high-insulin-spiking food with two servings of any low-insulin-spiking food.
   - **Plan I-B lunch meal:** Eat one serving of any high-insulin-spiking food with four servings of any low-insulin-spiking food.
   - **Plan I-C lunch meal:** Eat one serving of any high-insulin-spiking food with four servings of any low-insulin-spiking food.
2. Include foods high in omega-3 fats. Remember to limit trans and saturated fats.
3. Eat at least five servings of insulin-neutral foods each day at any time.
4. Include two to three servings of fruit each day. High-insulin-spiking fruits need to be linked. Nonlinking fresh fruits may be eaten at any time of day.

The food combination of your midday lunch meal achieves the following:

Nutritional Goal. This meal continues to supply your body with necessary carbohydrates and proteins needed for continued energy, bodybuilding, and repair.

Dietary fats are necessary for brain, nerve cells, and hormone production. They also provide valuable calories that are stored and used throughout the night to sustain vital body functions.

Metabolism Goal. Carbohydrates provide the fuel for cell functions. By linking and balancing them you prevent excessive sugar burning and cell acid buildup.

Hormone Goal. Avoiding insulin peaking not only improves insulin resistance but also regulates the stress hormone cortisol.

Neurotransmitter Goal. The protein contained in the low-insulin-spiking choice continues to provide the amino acids needed for making neurotransmitters.

Afternoon Serotonin-Boosting Snack

At approximately _____ : _____ P.M.

Eat this snack *at least three hours* after finishing lunch.

For all plans, choose one serving from the high-insulin-spiking foods. Remember that in order to make serotonin, you should not combine this snack with a low-insulin-spiking choice. Low-insulin-spiking choices are too high in protein and prevent the production of serotonin.

In the afternoon, the physical, mental, and emotional demands of your day start draining your serotonin reserves. Keep replacing serotonin throughout the day. This helps you avoid appetite and craving challenges that commonly occur in the late afternoon and evening when serotonin is at its lowest point.

If your serotonin levels have dropped significantly since morning, you will typically crave sweet or starchy carbohydrates around 3:00 each afternoon. If you tend to eat large food portions and graze on carbohydrates throughout the evening, this means you are not making enough serotonin early enough in the day. Ensure that you will have enough serotonin available by evening by remembering to include all of your serotonin-boosting snacks throughout the day, even if you don't feel too hungry.

Evening Dinner Meal

At approximately _____ : _____ P.M.

Before eating dinner, drink another eight ounces of Super pH Water.

1. Choose one of the following plans:
   - **Plan I-A dinner meal:** Eat one serving of a high-insulin-spiking food with two servings of low-insulin-spiking foods.
   - **Plan I-B dinner meal:** Eat one serving of any high-insulin-spiking food with four servings of low-insulin-spiking foods.
   - **Plan I-C dinner meal:** Eat one serving of any high-insulin-spiking food with four servings of low-insulin-spiking foods.
2. Remember to complete your daily requirement for omega-3 fats and minimize the amount of trans and saturated fats.
3. Eat insulin-neutral foods as desired at any time.
4. Eat two to three servings of fruits each day. Link high-insulin-spiking fruits.

The food combination of your evening meal achieves the following:

Nutritional Goal. The evening meal continues to supply you with the carbohydrate and protein nutrients necessary for sustaining your energy and repairing your body. Dietary fats are necessary by this time in order to provide the energy you need through the night when you are fast asleep.

Metabolism Goal. Carbohydrates continue to provide fuel for cell work, yet excessive amounts of glucose are avoided. Cell acid wastes are minimized.

Hormone Goal. Insulin peaking is well regulated by linking and balancing. In this way, the stress hormones do not overreact.

Neurotransmitter Goal. The protein contained in your low-insulin-spiking food choice provides the amino acids for making neurotransmitters.

Evening Serotonin-Boosting Snack

At approximately _____ : _____ P.M.

Eat your evening snack *at least three hours* after finishing your evening meal.

For all plans, choose one serving from the high-insulin-spiking foods. Remember that in order to make serotonin, you should not combine this snack with a low-insulin-spiking choice. Low-insulin-spiking choices are too high in protein and prevent serotonin production.

It is important for your brain to continue making serotonin throughout the evening and into the night. Serotonin converts to the sleep hormone melatonin. People who have difficulty getting to sleep or staying asleep are serotonin deficient. The brain normally replaces serotonin around 2:00 or 3:00 A.M. while you sleep. Once you get caught with chronic insomnia, it can be very difficult to get back into a normal sleeping pattern. Restoring levels of serotonin will help you break this vicious cycle. Some people take a melatonin supplement before going to bed. A better idea would be to replace the missing serotonin. This way you could improve other conditions caused by low serotonin while still increasing your melatonin.

Even though you are closely following these dietary recommendations, you still might not be producing enough serotonin. This is most likely due to the effects of stress on your hormones and neurotransmitter production. You will know you are still serotonin deficient because you may still have some difficulty controlling your appetite, cravings, and moods.

The more overweight and insulin resistant you are, the less helpful carbohydrate foods may be in helping you transport tryptophan to make serotonin. This blunted response helps explain why many overweight individuals feel the urge to eat lots of carbohydrates in attempts to make more serotonin. They require more than the normal amount of carbohydrates to raise their serotonin levels. The problems with eating large amounts of carbohydrates, of course, are that the excess calories cause weight gain and the abnormal insulin spiking worsens insulin resistance.

If you feel as though you are not getting enough serotonin by eating the serotonin-boosting snacks, you will need to add daily supplements to make more. This method, called neurotransmitter precursor therapy, offers a rapid, convenient, efficient, and safe way to boost your neurotransmitter production. It is described in detail as Plan II in Chapters 10 and 13.

Summary of Feel-Good Diet Plans I-A, I-B, and I-C

The following describes the Feel-Good-Diet Plan I summarized by plan rather than by meal.

Plan I-A

This plan works best for most women for weight loss. It has approximately 1,100 to 1,200 calories per day. If you exercise vigorously almost every day, use Plan B.

Before breakfast: Start with one serving of Super pH Water before breakfast.

Breakfast: Eat one high-insulin-spiking food serving with two low-insulin-spiking food servings.

Midmorning snack: Eat one high-insulin-spiking food as a serotonin-boosting snack.

Lunch: Have one serving of Super pH Water before lunch. Eat one high-insulin-spiking food serving with two low-insulin-spiking food servings.

Afternoon snack: Eat one high-insulin-spiking food as a serotonin-boosting snack.

Dinner: Have one serving of Super pH Water before your meal. Eat one high-insulin-spiking food serving with two low-insulin-spiking food servings.

Evening snack: Eat one high-insulin-spiking food as a serotonin-boosting snack.

Remember to include at least five servings a day of insulin-neutral foods. Also eat two to three servings of fruits each day.

Plan I-B

This plan works well for weight loss for most men and for women who are just beginning a muscle-building exercise routine or who are exercising several hours daily. It has about 1,400 to 1,500 calories per day.

Before breakfast: Start with a serving of Super pH Water before breakfast.

Breakfast: Eat one high-insulin-spiking food serving with two low-insulin-spiking food servings.

Midmorning snack: Eat one high-insulin-spiking food as a serotonin-boosting snack.

Lunch: Have one serving of Super pH Water before lunch. Eat one high-insulin-spiking food serving with four low-insulin-spiking food servings.

Afternoon snack: Eat one high-insulin-spiking food as a serotonin-boosting snack.

Dinner: Have one serving of Super pH Water before dinner. Eat one high-insulin-spiking food serving with four low-insulin-spiking food servings.

Evening snack: Eat one high-insulin-spiking food as a serotonin-boosting snack.

Remember to include at least five servings a day of insulin-neutral foods. Also eat two to three servings of fruits each day.

Plan I-C

This plan works well for weight loss for men who exercise several hours daily or who are just beginning a muscle-building exercise routine. It has about 1,600 to 1,800 calories per day.

Before breakfast: Start with a serving of Super pH Water before breakfast.

Breakfast: Eat two high-insulin-spiking food servings with four low-insulin-spiking food servings.

Midmorning snack: Eat one high-insulin-spiking food as a serotonin-boosting snack.

Lunch: Have one serving of Super pH Water before your meal. Eat one high-insulin-spiking food serving with four low-insulin-spiking food servings.

Afternoon snack: Eat one high-insulin-spiking food as a serotonin-boosting snack.

Dinner: Have one serving of Super pH Water before dinner. Eat one high-insulin-spiking food serving with four low-insulin-spiking food servings.

Evening snack: Eat one high-insulin-spiking food as a serotonin-boosting snack.

Remember to include at least five servings a day of insulin-neutral foods. Also eat two to three servings of fruits each day.

Insulin-Spiking Food Lists

The following food lists are divided into high-insulin-spiking, low-insulin-spiking, insulin-neutral, and nonlinking fresh fruit groups. Portion sizes are given for each single serving.

High-Insulin-Spiking Foods

You can estimate portions without actually having to weigh and measure. You will notice that most of the high-insulin-spiking foods, other than the sugary foods, have a portion size of approximately one-half cup. In order to estimate a half-cup serving, try to imagine if the piece of fruit, for example, would fit into a half-cup measuring cup. A half-cup serving when flattened out is approximately the size and thickness of the palm of a woman's hand or four fingers of a man's hand.

Italicized foods are higher in fat content.

Fruits

Food or Beverage	Serving Size
Apple chips	9 chips
Apple juice	½ cup
Apples, dried, sulfured	3 slices

Food or Beverage	Serving Size
Applesauce	
Sweetened	⅓ cup
Unsweetened	½ cup
Apricots	
Canned in heavy syrup	¼ cup (including syrup)
Canned in juice	½ cup (including syrup)
Dried halves	7 halves
Apricot nectar, canned	½ cup
Banana	½ small (8¾-inch length) *or* ¾ cup
Blueberries	
Fresh	¾ cup
Frozen, sweetened	⅓ cup
Cantaloupe	⅓ of a 5-inch-diameter melon
Cranberry juice, light	1 cup
Cranberry juice cocktail	⅓ cup
Cranberry-apple juice	½ cup
Cranberry sauce	2 tablespoons
Dates, whole	2½ dates
Fig, dried	1 fig
Fruit cocktail	
In heavy syrup	¼ cup
In juice	½ cup
Grapefruit juice	
Sweetened	½ cup
Unsweetened	¾ cup
Grapes, green or red, fresh	17 grapes
Grape juice	
Sweetened	⅓ cup
100 percent	⅓ cup
Light	1 cup
Honeydew melon	⅛ of a 6½-inch-diameter melon
Kiwifruit, fresh	1½ kiwifruits
Mango, fresh	½ mango

Food or Beverage	Serving Size
Orange, fresh	1 small (3-inch diameter) *or* ½ of a large (6-inch diameter)
Mandarin sections, canned in light syrup	⅓ cup (including syrup)
Orange juice	½ cup
Orange-grapefruit juice	¾ cup
Papaya, fresh	1 cup
Peach	
Canned in heavy syrup	¼ cup (including syrup)
Canned in juice	½ cup (including juice)
Frozen, sweetened	¼ cup
Pear	
Canned in heavy syrup	¼ cup (including syrup)
Canned in juice	½ cup (including juice)
Dried halves	1 half
Pineapple	
Fresh, chunks	¾ cup
Canned in heavy syrup:	
Crushed, chunks, tidbits	¼ cup (including syrup)
Slices	1½ slices
Canned in juice:	
Crushed, chunks, tidbits	⅓ cup (including syrup)
Slices	1½ slices
Pineapple juice, unsweetened	½ cup
Plums	
Canned in heavy syrup	¼ cup (including syrup) *or* 2 without syrup
Canned in juice	½ cup (including juice) *or* 3 without juice
Prunes	3 prunes
Prune juice	⅓ cup
Raisins	¾ ounce
Raspberries	
Fresh	1 cup
Frozen, sweetened	¼ cup

Food or Beverage	Serving Size
Strawberries	
Fresh	1½ cups
Frozen, sweetened	¼ cup
Tangerine	1½ tangerines
Watermelon, cubed	1½ cups

Baked Goods

Food	Serving Size
Bagel	⅓ (3½-inch diameter) *or* ⅕ (5½-inch diameter)
Biscuit (reduced fat recommended)	1 (3-inch diameter)
Bread crumbs, dry	¼ cup
Bread crumbs, soft	⅔ cup
Bread cubes, soft	1 cup
Breads (toasted breads are the same portions)	
Boston brown bread (3¼-inch diameter)	⅓-inch slice
Cracked wheat, multigrain, oatmeal, white, raisin, or whole wheat (1-pound loaf with 18 slices)	1 slice
Deli-style breads as already listed and including:	
French, Italian, Vienna, potato, and rye (1½-pound loaf with 18 slices)	⅔ slice
French bread baguette (2-inch diameter)	1¼-inch slice
Bread stuffing	⅓ cup
Cakes	
Angel food (9¾-inch tube cake)	1/20 of cake
Frosted double-layer devil's food, white, or yellow (8- or 9-inch diameter)	1/40 of cake

Food	Serving Size
Unfrosted cakes (8- or 9-inch diameter)	⅟₂₅ of cake
Carrot cake with cream cheese frosting, single layer	1 piece (2-by-1½ inches)
Fruitcake	⅓-inch slice
Pound cake (8½-by-3½-by-3¼-inch loaf)	⅟₁₇ of loaf (½-inch slice)
Cheesecake (9-inch diameter)	⅟₂₄ of cake
Cookies and bars	
Brownie, frosted	1 (1½-by-1¾-by-1-inch piece)
Chocolate chip cookie (2¼-inch diameter)	½ cookie
Fig bar	1 cookie
Oatmeal raisin cookie (3-inch diameter)	½ cookie
Peanut butter cookie (3-inch diameter)	½ cookie
Sugar cookie (2½-inch diameter)	½ cookie
Vanilla wafers	5 cookies
Corn chips	1 ounce
Crackers	
Small cheese crackers	25 crackers
Graham crackers	3 squares
Matzo	⅔ matzo
Melba toast	4 pieces
Saltines	7 crackers
Ritz crackers	7 crackers
Wheat Thins	12 crackers
Croissant (4½-by-4-by-1¾-inch size)	½ croissant
Danish pastry	1 ounce
Doughnuts	
Cake type, plain (3¼-inch diameter)	½ doughnut
Yeast leavened, glazed (3¾-inch diameter)	½ doughnut
English muffin	½ muffin
Muffins (2½-inch diameter), any flavor	¾ muffin
Pancakes (4-inch diameter)	2 pancakes

Food	Serving Size

Pies (9-inch diameter)
    Fruit pie — 1 wedge, 1-inch wide at crust edge
    Cream pie — 1 wedge, 1-inch wide at crust edge
    Lemon meringue pie — 1 wedge, 1-inch wide at crust edge
    Pecan pie — 1 wedge, 1-inch wide at crust edge
    Pumpkin pie — 1 wedge, 1-inch wide at crust edge
    Individual snack pies — ½ pie

Pretzels
    Thin sticks (2¼-inch length) — 63 pretzels
    Dutch twists (2¾-by-2⅝-inch size) — 1 pretzel
    Thin twists (3¼-by-2¼-inch size) — 3 pretzels
    Soft pretzels (6-by-5-inch size) — ⅕ pretzel

Rolls and buns
    Dinner roll (2½-inch diameter) — ¾ roll
    Hot dog bun — ¾ bun
    Hamburger bun — ⅔ bun
    Hard roll (3¾-inch diameter) — ½ roll
    Submarine roll — 3-inch piece

Toaster pastry — ½ pastry

Taco shells — 2 shells

Tortilla
    Corn (6-inch diameter) — 1 tortilla
    Flour (8-inch diameter) — 1 tortilla

Waffles (7-inch diameter) — ½ waffle

Grain Products

Food	Serving Size

Barley, cooked — ⅓ cup

Breakfast cereals, cooked
    Grits or hominy — ½ cup
    Cream of Wheat — ½ cup
    Mix-and-eat packet, plain — ¾ packet
    Malt-O-Meal — ½ cup
    Oatmeal — ½ cup

Food	Serving Size
Instant oatmeal, from packet	
Plain	1 packet
Flavored	½ packet
Multigrain cereal	⅔ cup
Breakfast cereals, ready to eat	
40 percent bran flakes	½ cup
Corn flakes	¾ cup
General Mills Cheerios	1 cup
General Mills Golden Grahams	½ cup
General Mills Total	½ cup
General Mills Trix	⅔ cup
General Mills Wheaties	⅔ cup
Granola	⅕ cup
Kellogg's All-Bran	¼ cup
Kellogg's Froot Loops	⅔ cup
Kellogg's Frosted Flakes	½ cup
Kellogg's Product 19	½ cup
Kellogg's Raisin Bran	¼ cup
Kellogg's Rice Krispies	⅔ cup
Kellogg's Special K	1 cup
Kellogg's Sugar Smacks	½ cup
Nabisco Shredded Wheat	½ cup
Post Golden Crisp	½ cup
Post Grape Nuts	¼ cup
Post Raisin Bran	⅓ cup
Quaker Cap'n Crunch	½ cup
Quaker Puffed Rice	1¼ cups
Bulgur	⅓ cup
Macaroni	½ cup
Pasta	
Egg noodles, cooked	½ cup
Chow mein, dry	½ cup
Spaghetti, fettuccine, vermicelli, and all other pastas	½ cup
Popcorn (unbuttered recommended)	
Air popped or low fat	5 cups
Popped in oil	2½ cups
Caramel coated	½ cup

Food	Serving Size
Rice	
Brown	⅓ cup
White	⅓ cup
Instant	⅓ cup
Wild	⅓ cup
Wheat germ	
Raw	½ cup
Toasted	¼ cup

Sugary Foods and Sweets

Food	Serving Size
Apple butter	2 tablespoons
Caramel	⅔ ounce
Chocolate	
Plain	1 ounce
With almonds	1 ounce
With peanuts	1½ ounces
With rice cereal	¾ ounce
Chocolate chips	2½ tablespoons
Fondant candies (mints, caramel corn, etc.)	½ ounce
Fudge	¾ ounce
Gumdrops	⅔ ounce
Hard candies, all flavors	½ ounce
Jelly beans	½ ounce
Marshmallows	
Large	3 each
Small	⅓ cup
Custard, baked with sugar	½ cup
Gelatin	
Regular	½ cup
Sugar free	Unlimited

Food	Serving Size
Honey	1 tablespoon
Jam, jelly, or preserves	1 tablespoon
Popsicle (2-ounce size)	1 Popsicle
Sugar	
Brown or white	4 teaspoons
Powdered	2½ tablespoons
Syrups	
Corn syrup	1 tablespoon
Chocolate, thin type	1⅓ tablespoons
Chocolate, fudge type	1⅓ tablespoons
Maple syrup	
Regular	1 tablespoon
Light or reduced calorie	2 tablespoons
Molasses	1 tablespoon

Alcoholic Beverages

Beverage	Serving Size
Beer	12 ounces
Dessert wine	4 ounces
Alcoholic beverages made with fruit or sugary mixers (daiquiries or margaritas)	4 ounces
Liqueurs	2 ounces

Most alcoholic drinks such as wine, whiskey, gin, and vodka are not high in carbohydrates and do not need to be considered high-insulin-spiking foods. They should be limited to eight ounces per week, however, in a weight-loss plan.

Soda Pop

Beverage	Serving Size
All varieties except sugar free	4 ounces

Low-Insulin-Spiking Foods

A one-ounce serving is approximately the volume of two fingers. A two-ounce serving is approximately the volume of a deck of cards.

Fish and Shellfish

Food	Serving Size
Clams	1½ ounces
Crab meat	1 ounce
Fish sticks (low-fat variety recommended)	1 stick
Herring, pickled	1 ounce
Oysters	
Fresh	⅓ cup
Cooked	1 ounce
Lobster meat	1 ounce
Salmon, canned, broiled, baked without added fat, smoked, or *fried*	1 ounce
Sardines, packed in oil	1 ounce
Sardines, packed in mustard, barbecue sauce, etc.	1 ounce
Shrimp, cooked, canned, or *fried*	1 ounce
Trout, broiled, baked without added fat, or *fried*	1 ounce
Tuna, packed in water	1 ounce
Tuna, packed in oil	1 ounce
Whitefish, steamed, poached, baked without added fat, or *fried* (cod, flounder, sole, haddock, halibut, perch, pollock)	1 ounce

Beef, Pork, or Lamb

Food	Serving Size
Sirloin, top round, London broil, or flank cuts; braised, roasted, broiled, grilled, or *fried*	1 ounce
All other cuts	1 ounce
Ground beef	
Less than 10 percent fat	1 ounce
Regular, lean, or extra lean	1 ounce
Heart	1 ounce
Liver	1 ounce
Tongue	1 ounce
Beef jerky	½ ounce
Corned beef	1 ounce
Chipped beef	1 ounce

Poultry

Food	Serving Size
Chicken or turkey	
White meat without skin, broiled, roasted, baked, boiled, or *fried*	1 ounce
White meat with skin	1 ounce
Dark meat with or without skin	1 ounce
Chicken or turkey liver	1 ounce
Duck, Cornish game hen	1 ounce
Ostrich or emu	1 ounce
Pheasant, cooked without skin	1 ounce

Processed Meats

Food	Serving Size
Bologna	
Beef and pork or turkey	2 pieces
Fat free	2 pieces
Braunschweiger or liverwurst	2 ounces
Breakfast sausage, pork or turkey, links or patties	1 ounce
Ham	
Picnic	1 ounce
97 percent lean or leaner	1 ounce
Hot dogs or franks	
Regular beef, pork, chicken, or turkey	1½ franks
97 percent lean or leaner	1½ franks
Pepperoni	
Regular, sliced	17 pieces
Reduced fat	17 pieces
Salami	
Luncheon meat	2 ounces
Dry	1 ounce
Sandwich spread, pork and beef	6 tablespoons
Vienna sausages, pork and beef or turkey	4 sausages

Dried Beans, Legumes, Nuts, and Seeds

Food	Serving Size
Cooked, dried bean (all kinds), lentils, or split peas	⅓ cup
Chili con carne	⅓ cup
Refried beans	⅓ cup
Hummus	⅓ cup
Baked beans	⅓ cup

Food	Serving Size
Cashews, Brazil nuts, almonds, and English walnuts	1½ ounces
Macadamia nuts	3 ounces
Peanuts	1 ounce
Peanut butter	2 tablespoons
Pecans	3 ounces
Pine nuts	2 ounces
Pistachio nuts, shelled	1½ ounces
Pumpkin kernels	1 ounce
Sunflower seeds, shelled	¼ cup
Tahini (sesame butter)	2 tablespoons
Black walnuts	1 ounce

Dairy/Egg Products

Food	Serving Size
Buttermilk	8 fluid ounces
Cheese	
Cheddar, blue, Brie, Camembert, Edam, Gouda, Gruyère, Gorgonzola, Muenster, Monterey Jack, Parmesan, Romano, Swiss, American	1 ounce
Fat-free cheeses already listed	1 ounce
Mozzarella, part skim or nonfat	1 ounce
Cottage cheese	
Creamed	¼ cup
2 percent, 1 percent, or nonfat	¼ cup
Dry curd	⅓ cup
Cream cheese, nonfat only*	3 tablespoons
Custard, baked with no added sugar**	½ cup

*(Reduced-fat or regular cream cheeses do not have adequate protein.)

(Custards made with sugar **must be counted as a high-insulin-spiking food.)

Food	Serving Size
Eggs, whole	1 egg
Egg whites	2 egg whites
Egg substitutes	¼ cup
Ice cream, frozen yogurt, ice milk*** with no sugar added, low-fat or fat free	8 fluid ounces
Pudding, sugar free made with 1 percent or nonfat milk****	1 cup
Ricotta cheese	
Made with whole milk	¼ cup
Made with part skim	¼ cup
Milk	
Nonfat or 1 percent	8 fluid ounces
2 percent or whole	8 fluid ounces
Nonfat dried milk	⅓ cup (dry)
Evaporated milk	
Whole	4 fluid ounces
Skim	4 fluid ounces
Goat milk	8 fluid ounces
Soy milk*****	8 fluid ounces
Yogurt, plain	1 cup
Yogurt, flavored, no sugar added, nonfat or low-fat, labeled as "Lite" or "Light"******	1 cup

***(Regular frozen milk desserts that contain sugar **must** be counted as a high-insulin-spiking food.)

****(Regular puddings that contain sugar **must** be counted as a high-insulin-spiking food.)

*****(Chocolate milk, eggnog, malted milk, milkshakes, and other flavored milks that contain sugar **must** be counted as high-insulin-spiking foods unless sugar free.)

******(Yogurts with sugar added **must** be counted as high-insulin-spiking foods.)

Insulin-Neutral Foods

All vegetables or plants not found on either the high- or low-insulin-spiking food lists are insulin-neutral foods.

You can eat unlimited amounts of vegetables in this group as well as tomatoes and avocados. Tomatoes and avocados are really fruits, yet most of us think of them as vegetables.

Nonlinking Fresh Fruits

These fruits can be considered very low-insulin-spiking foods *only* when eaten in fresh forms. They can be eaten at any time without having to link them to a protein.

If these fruits undergo *any* processing, drying, sweetening, mashing, grinding, juicing, or cooking, their fiber and sugar structures change. They then markedly raise insulin and need to be considered high-insulin-spiking foods.

Fruit	Serving Size
Apple, fresh	1 small (3-inch diameter) *or* ½ of a large (6-inch diameter)
Apricots, fresh	4 apricots
Cherries, sweet, fresh	14 cherries
Grapefruit, fresh	½ of a small (6-inch diameter)
Lemon, fresh	1 medium
Lime, fresh	1 medium
Peach, fresh	1 small (3-inch diameter) *or* ½ of a large (6-inch diameter)
Pear, fresh	1 small (3-inch diameter) *or* ½ of a large (6-inch diameter)
Plum, fresh	2 medium (2⅛-inch diameter) *or* 4 small (1½-inch diameter)
Nectarine, fresh	1 small (3-inch diameter) *or* ½ of a large (6-inch diameter)

Mixed Dishes and Fast-Foods List

The following foods contain combinations of *both* high- and low-insulin-spiking foods. *Italicized foods* are higher in fat content.

Beef or chicken stew (1 cup) = two servings of low-insulin-spiking foods **and** one serving of high-insulin-spiking foods

Beef or chicken pot pie (7 ounces) = three servings of low-insulin-spiking foods **and** two servings of high-insulin-spiking foods

Chicken and noodles (1 cup) = three servings of low-insulin-spiking foods **and** two servings of high-insulin-spiking foods

French toast (1 piece) = one serving of low-insulin-spiking foods **and** one serving of high-insulin-spiking foods

Macaroni and cheese (boxed) (1 cup) = one serving of low-insulin-spiking foods **and** two servings of high-insulin-spiking foods

Spaghetti (canned) (1 cup) = one serving of low-insulin-spiking foods **and** two servings of high-insulin-spiking foods

Cheeseburger (regular) = two servings of low-insulin-spiking foods **and** two servings of high-insulin-spiking foods

Cheeseburger (quarter-pound patty) = four servings of low-insulin-spiking foods **and** two servings of high-insulin-spiking foods

Burrito (beef and bean) = three servings of low-insulin-spiking foods **and** three servings of high-insulin-spiking foods

Breaded chicken sandwich = three servings of low-insulin-spiking foods **and** two servings of high-insulin-spiking foods

Corn dog = one serving of low-insulin-spiking foods **and** two servings of high-insulin-spiking foods

English muffin with egg, cheese, and bacon = two servings of low-insulin-spiking foods **and** two servings of high-insulin-spiking foods

Fish sandwich = two servings of low-insulin-spiking foods **and** two servings of high-insulin-spiking foods

Hamburger with bun (regular) = two servings of low-insulin-spiking foods **and** two servings of high-insulin-spiking foods

Hamburger with bun (quarter-pound patty) = three servings of low-insulin-spiking foods **and** two servings of high-insulin-spiking foods

Pizza, ⅛ of 15-inch round pizza, plain cheese (thin crust) = two servings of low-insulin-spiking foods **and** two servings of high-insulin-spiking foods

Pizza, ⅛ of 15-inch round pizza, plain cheese (thick crust) = two servings of low-insulin-spiking foods **and** four servings of high-insulin-spiking foods

Roast beef sandwich = three servings of low-insulin-spiking foods **and** two servings of high-insulin-spiking foods

Taco = one serving of low-insulin-spiking foods **and** one serving of high-insulin-spiking foods

Fast-Food Choices

You can eat fast food and still follow a good eating plan. All of these meal suggestions fit into our plans only as indicated. If an item is not listed for a plan, choose a different item. Coffee, diet sodas, or water can be added to any meal.

Arby's

Sourdough Egg and Cheese without half of the bread fits Plan A or B.

Regular Roast Beef without half of the bun and with 2 percent (or lower-fat) milk fits Plan B or C.

Junior Roast Beef without half of the bun fits Plan A. Have two but take off half of the buns for Plan B or C.

Roast Chicken Club without half of the bun fits Plan B or C.

Market Fresh Roast Ham and Swiss without mayonnaise on a wrap works great for Plan B or C.

Market Fresh Roast Turkey and Swiss without mayonnaise on a wrap fits Plan B or C.

Martha's Vineyard Salad fits Plan B or C. Choose the light buttermilk ranch or raspberry vinaigrette dressing.

Arby's sauce, honey mustard, Horsey Sauce, ketchup, light mayonnaise, marinara, red ranch, or three-pepper sauce can be added to any sandwich.

Burger King

Add a Side Garden Salad with garden ranch dressing or sweet onion vinaigrette to any sandwich to complete your meal.

Whopper Jr. without the mayo and half of the bun fits Plan A.

Have a Low-Carb Whopper Jr.—double it and add apple juice for Plan B or C.

Low-Carb Whopper Jr. with Cheese with apple juice fits Plan A.

Hamburger without half of the bun fits Plan A.

Have a Low-Carb Angus Steak Burger or Low-Carb Chicken Whopper—and add apple juice for Plan B or C.

Six-piece Chicken Tenders works for Plan A.

Ketchup in small amounts can be added to any sandwich.

Tendergrill Chicken Caesar Salad or Tendergrill Chicken Garden Salad with garden ranch, creamy garlic Caesar, sweet onion vinaigrette, or tomato balsamic vinaigrette dressings and garlic Parmesan toast will fit Plan B or C.

Croissan'wich with ham, egg, and cheese minus half of the croissant will fit Plan A.

Carl's Junior

Add a Garden Salad with fat-free Italian dressing to make a meal out of any sandwich.

Jr. Hamburger minus half of the bun fits Plan A.

Low-Carb Charbroiled Chicken Club sandwich works for Plan B or C.

Charbroiled Chicken Salad fits well for Plan B or C. Use fat-free Italian dressing.

Buffalo wing sauce or house sauce in small amounts can be added to any sandwich.

Dairy Queen

Complete your meal with a side salad with fat-free Italian, reduced-calorie buttermilk, or fat-free ranch dressing.

DQ Homestyle Burger or Grilled Chicken Sandwich without half of the bun fits Plan A.

Grilled Chicken Salad with a DQ No Sugar Added Fudge Bar is a treat for Plan B or C. Use the same dressings listed earlier.

Domino's Pizza

Have ⅛ of a 12-inch medium pizza with crunchy thin crust and any single meat topping and unlimited vegetable toppings along with two barbecue or hot buffalo wings for Plan A. Make it four buffalo wings for Plan B or C.

Jack in the Box

Add a side salad without croutons with low-fat balsamic dressing to your sandwich to make it a complete meal.

Hamburger without half the bun fits Plan A.

Breakfast Jack minus half the bread fits Plan A.

Asian Chicken Salad with wontons and low-fat balsamic dressing works for Plan A.

Chicken Caesar Salad with croutons or Southwest Chicken Salad with Spicy Corn Sticks and low-fat balsamic dressing works for Plan B or C.

Soy sauce, Frank's Red Hot Buffalo Dipping Sauce, reduced-fat herb mayo, or taco sauce may be added to any sandwich or salad.

Kentucky Fried Chicken

Add green beans, coleslaw, a Caesar side salad without croutons, or a house side salad to make a complete meal. Use Hidden Valley Fat Free Ranch Dressing or Hidden Valley Golden Italian Light Dressing.

Roasted Caesar Salad or Roasted BLT Salad with Hidden Valley Fat Free Ranch or Hidden Valley Golden Italian Light Dressing and Parmesan garlic croutons are good options for Plan B or C.

Tender Roast Fillet Meal is a good choice for Plan B or C if you leave half of the rice on your plate.

Tender Roast Sandwich without sauce works for Plan B or C.

KFC Original Chicken Breast without skin along with any one of the following choices can be included in Plan B or C: small mashed potatoes with or without gravy, or corn on the cob, or potato salad, or baked beans.

McDonald's

Add a side salad without croutons, with low-fat balsamic vinaigrette or low-fat family recipe Italian dressing to make your meal complete. Iced tea can be added to any meal.

Hamburger without half of the bun fits Plan A.

Six-piece Chicken McNuggets or two pieces of Chicken Selects Premium Breast Strips work for Plan A. Ask for hot mustard sauce or spicy buffalo sauce.

Bacon Ranch, Caesar, or California Cobb Salads with grilled chicken with croutons and the dressings listed earlier fit in Plan B or C. Or leave out the croutons and substitute Apple Dippers without the caramel.

Egg McMuffin without half of the muffin works for Plan A. Add a side of scrambled eggs for Plan B or C.

Subway

Add a Veggie Delite salad without croutons with fat-free Italian dressing to make your sandwich a complete meal.

Ham, roast beef, turkey breast, or turkey breast and ham on a wrap work for Plan A. Ask for double meat for Plan B or C.

Club or roasted chicken or sweet onion chicken teriyaki or cheese steak or Subway melt on a wrap can be included in Plan B or C even without double meat.

Grilled chicken and spinach salad or club salad with croutons and with fat-free Italian dressing work for Plan A. Add chili con carne for Plan B or C.

Or just order two bowls of chili con carne and some saltines if you are on Plan B or C.

Two bowls of minestrone or roasted chicken noodle soup can be included in Plan A.

Breakfast deli round with cheese with only half of the bun will work for Plan A.

Breakfast wrap with cheese or breakfast wrap with honey mustard ham and egg or a western breakfast wrap with cheese will work for Plan B or C.

Taco Bell

Ask for all items to be Fresco Style.

One Crunchy Taco, Soft Beef Taco, Ranchero Chicken Soft Taco, Spicy Chicken Taco, or Grilled Steak Soft Taco with a side of Pintos 'n Cheese can be included in Plan A. Add two sides of Pintos 'n Cheese for Plan B or C.

Wendy's

Add a side salad with reduced-fat creamy ranch or house vinaigrette dressing to make a complete meal out of a sandwich.

Junior hamburger, junior cheeseburger, or a junior smoky cheddarburger with only half of the bun fits Plan A.

Mandarin Chicken Salad without crispy noodles and with reduced-fat creamy ranch or house vinaigrette dressing works for Plan B or C.

Spring Mix Salad with house vinaigrette dressing or reduced-fat creamy ranch dressing and a mandarin orange cup fits Plan A.

A small chili with three packages of saltines or one serving of low-fat strawberry-flavored yogurt can be used for Plan A.

Make it a large chili with shredded cheddar cheese for Plan B or C.

Using Food Labels for Linking and Balancing

You can approximate correct link-and-balance portion sizes of any packaged food just by checking nutrition labels. One serving of a high-insulin-spiking food contains 15 grams of carbohydrates. You will first need to subtract the fiber and sugar alcohol amounts from the total amount of carbohydrates listed. The difference is the amount of carbohydrates you need to consider when linking and balancing.

Each 15-gram serving of a high-insulin-spiking food needs to link with 7 grams of protein, the amount in a single serving of a low-insulin-spiking food choice. The protein listing on the food label will automatically tell you how much protein is contained in that food.

Quick Food Label Reference

One serving of a high-insulin-spiking choice contains 15 grams of carbohydrates. (Remember to subtract the fiber and sugar alcohol.)

One serving of a low-insulin-spiking choice contains 7 grams of protein.

Main Points in Chapter 7

- The Feel-Good Diet Plan I combines foods in ways that optimize both insulin control and serotonin production.

- Foods containing more than 12 percent protein inhibit serotonin production.

- The meals in the Link-and-Balance Method control your insulin; the snacks increase your serotonin.

- The timing and portions of your meals and snacks are important when trying to both control insulin and produce serotonin.

8

The Different Kinds of Dietary Fats

Certain dietary fats are critical for proper brain function and neurotransmitter production. Your brain is formed mainly from fats you get in food. Nerve cell membranes are also composed of fat. Neurons need cholesterol and other fats to function properly. The most important dietary fats for the brain are the omega-3 and omega-6 essential fatty acids.

Essential fats are those that must be obtained through food; the body cannot make them. We must eat them often in our foods or we develop essential fatty acid deficiencies. Common signs of such deficiencies include dry skin, dry hair, dry eyes, constipation, and small dry skin bumps on the upper arms or thighs. We now realize that deficiencies of essential fatty acids can cause other symptoms such as cravings for fats and changes in mood. Essential fatty acids are necessary for the formation of healthy cell membranes, proper development and functioning of the brain and nerves, and production of hormonelike substances called *eicosanoids* (thromboxanes, leukotrienes, prostaglandins). Eicosanoids regulate many body functions including blood pressure, blood thickness (viscosity), and blood vessel constriction (vasoconstriction) as well as immune and inflammatory responses.

There are two kinds of essential fatty acids: omega-3 and omega-6 fatty acids. Omega-6 fatty acids are common in the American diet. They are found in vegetable oils and all foods made with vegetable oils such as salad dressings, margarines, and baked goods. Omega-3 fatty acids, on the other hand, are not as common in our diets. They are found in fish oils and some nuts and seeds. It is important to include both types of essential fatty acids often in your diet. If you eat an excessive amount of one type and not much of the other, you are more likely to show signs of deficiencies.

Omega-3 Essential Fatty Acids

Alpha-linolenic acid (ALA) is the precursor to the omega-3 fatty acids. Originating from the sea, ALA is found in phytoplankton, algae, and green leafy vegetables. Linolenic acid (LNA) evolved from ALA and is found in flaxseeds, walnuts, canola oil, soybeans, and soy products. Our bodies convert plant forms of omega-3s into animal forms called *eicosapentaenoic acid* (*EPA*) and *docosahexaenoic acid* (*DHA*). These omega-3 fats can also be found naturally in fish. The highest levels are found in fatty fishes such as herring, halibut, mackerel, salmon, trout, sardines, and oysters. Many recent studies have found that frequently eating fish reduces heart disease. Some studies show that the plant forms of omega-3 are also healthy for the heart, but the evidence is not as clear. For this reason, the American Heart Association recommends: "Americans with no history of heart disease eat at least two servings of fish each week as well as flax, canola, soy, walnuts, and green leafy vegetables or sea vegetables often." Those with heart disease are advised to eat fish daily or take a fish oil supplement. Many people are concerned about mercury contamination of fish. However, the benefits of omega-3s for adult men and adult women past childbearing age are definitely greater than the risk (americanheart.org).

Researchers suggest that 100 to 200 milligrams daily of DHA and 200 to 400 milligrams of EPA are adequate for most adults, although pregnant and nursing women need 50 percent more. An average serving of salmon contains 1 gram of EPA and 2 grams of DHA; the American Heart Association recommends at least two servings of fish per week, along with a limited intake of saturated fats. Those who want to relieve symptoms of depression may require as much as 5 to 10 grams daily.

Omega-3s are available in many forms. Liquid flaxseed oil contains mostly ALA. One tablespoon of flaxseed oil a day is recommended. Flaxseed oil does not remain potent if heated. It needs to be stored in the refrigerator, as it spoils easily. You can also grind two tablespoons of fresh flaxseeds daily in a coffee grinder and mix it in with any food. Many people enjoy it in their morning smoothies, cold cereal, or oatmeal. If you grind your flax ahead of time, keep it refrigerated and stored for only one week at a time. You can purchase fish oil capsules or concentrated omega-3 EPA/DHA capsules made with purified fish oils and plant oils at most vitamin counters.

Omega-6 Essential Fatty Acids

There are several omega-6 fatty acids, the most common being *linoleic acid* (*LA*). Don't confuse this with *linolenic acid* (*LNA*), which is an omega-3. Food sources of linoleic acid include sunflower, safflower, corn, and sesame oils. Cold-pressed oils contain the highest amounts of essential fatty acids. Heating and processing these fragile oils can damage them. The best sources for other omega-6 fats are *gamma linoleic acid* (*GLA*) found as primrose, borage, and black currant seed oils; and *arachidonic acid* (*AA*), which is plentiful in meat, eggs, and dairy products. We can also make arachidonic acid from linoleic acid in our bodies.

Experts recommend that you keep the amount of omega-6 fats you get from soft margarines and salad dressing oils made from vegetable oils (other than canola oil) to about two to six teaspoons each day.

Getting the Right Ratio of Omega-6 to Omega-3

A balanced ratio of the two fatty acid families is necessary for a healthy brain, which is structurally composed of a one-to-one ratio of omega-6 to omega-3 fats. American diets tend to have an abundance of omega-6 fats (from meats and dairy) producing ratios of twenty to one or higher. Researchers believe this imbalance leads to a variety of mental disorders, including hyperactivity, depression, and schizophrenia. A Dutch study of learning capabilities in males, ages sixty-nine to eighty-nine, suggests that those with a high intake of omega-6 fatty acids (found in red meat) were found to have lowered learning scores, while those consuming foods high in omega-3 oils showed improved brain function.

The ratio of these fats in the brain can be adjusted by the foods that are eaten. The Food and Nutrition Board of the National Institute of Medicine recommends that men eat 1.7 grams of linoleic acid (omega-6) and 1.6 grams of linolenic acid (omega-3) daily. Women should eat 1.2 grams of linoleic acid and 1.1 grams of linolenic acid each day. Currently in the United States, our daily intake of omega-3 fatty acids is only 100 milligrams.

Saturated and Trans Fats

Foods containing saturated and trans fats are especially harmful and should be kept to a minimum. Saturated animal fats, such as fatty meats, poultry skin, butter, and other high-fat dairy products, are associated with increases in heart disease.

The brain cells need a certain degree of flexibility to function properly. This is achieved by having different-sized fatty acid molecules lining the cell membrane. Normal fatty acids have a flexible curve to their shape. When these same fat molecules undergo certain food processes, they mutate into forms rarely found in nature, called trans fats. They become straighter and more rigid. These rigid fat molecules in the brain cell walls cause these cells to malfunction.

Food manufacturers hydrogenate liquid oils to form solid fats. Hydrogenated fats have a longer shelf life and are easier to work with. Unfortunately, this process forms trans fats. Trans fats are found in hard margarines and vegetable shortening. The most plentiful sources of trans fats in the American diet are baked goods made with hydrogenated fats. These include crackers, cookies, and other snack foods.

Studies suggest that trans fatty acids increase the risk of heart disease even more than do saturated fats. Dietary trans fatty acids also increase the risk of type 2 diabetes in women. Results of a Harvard University study correlated fourteen years of medical and dietary information from more than 84,000 women ages thirty-four to fifty-nine. Researchers found that the risk of type 2 diabetes rose by 39 percent simply by increasing trans fatty acids by 2 percent of the women's total daily calories.

In addition to increasing the risk of heart disease and type 2 diabetes, trans fats have also been associated with premature aging of the brain and increased cholesterol levels. Researchers find that trans fats lower the amount of "good" (HDL) cholesterol more than saturated fats do. Both trans and saturated fats increase the amount of LDL, the "bad" form of cholesterol.

Food labels include the trans fat content. Avoid all foods with hydrogenated fats listed as one of the main ingredients in the ingredient list. Most soft-tub margarines are now specially made *without* trans fats and should state "0 grams trans fats" in the Nutrition Facts area on the label. These are much better for you than hard margarines or butter. This is especially true if they are also good sources of omega-3 fatty acids.

"Happy" Fat: The Effect of Omega-3 Fats on Neurotransmitters

Studies link diets low in omega-3 fatty acids with growing rates of depression in the United States. In 1995, Joseph R. Hibbeln, M.D., a psychiatrist and biochemist from the National Institutes of Health, remarked, "We are eating ourselves into a collective depression by consuming the wrong sorts of fats . . . intensifying our vulnerability to depression."

Belgian researchers at Antwerp's University Hospital found that seriously depressed patients had lower omega-3 fatty acid levels than mildly depressed patients. People with low amounts of omega-3 in their spinal fluid have low levels of serotonin. Researchers at the University of British Columbia found that newborn piglets fed for eighteen days with a feed containing omega-3 fatty acids had twice as much serotonin in their brains as those on standard feed. Serotonin acts as a signal to guide migrating neurons to their correct location and also assists the correct growth of axons and dendrites. Lack of omega-3 fatty acids early in life may forever alter the way the brain develops and operates. Adding omega-3 fatty acids, especially DHA, to infant formula milk has been suggested by some nutritional experts.

Two large studies provide evidence that people who eat fish are less likely to become depressed. In 2001, a study of more than three thousand Finnish adults showed that those who ate more fish had a lower rate of depression. Countries where the population eats high amounts of fish, such as Japan, Korea, and Taiwan, have the lowest rates of depression, including the lowest rate of postpartum depression.

At a 1997 conference on nutrition and the brain, leading experts recognized that low levels of DHA (omega-3) were associated with certain neurological conditions. They highlighted studies that showed links among deficient DHA levels, hostility, and aggression. These are recognized characteristics of low serotonin levels.

How do omega-3 fats help depression? Studies also show that omega-3 fatty acids have mood-stabilizing and antidepressant effects. Twenty percent of our brain's weight consists of essential fatty acids. DHA, the main omega-3 fatty acid from fish, is the most abundant fat in the brain. One theory is that omega-3s increase serotonin in the synapses. Another theory is that they improve the nerve impulse once neurotransmitters dock onto their receptors.

In the 1990s, Andrew Stoll of Harvard University conducted a study on patients with bipolar disorders. After four months, those given high doses of fish oil capsules had significantly longer breaks from their depression than those on placebo.

In another study, a team from Sheffield University gave large omega-3 doses to depressed patients who hadn't been helped by drugs such as Prozac. At twelve weeks, 69 percent showed marked improvement compared with 25 percent of those given placebos.

Boris Nemets and colleagues from Ben Gurion University in Israel reported that depressed patients who were not responding to drugs showed significant progress within two weeks of taking fish oil. By week four, more than half of the subjects taking fish oil had a 50 percent decline in symptoms such as low mood, insomnia, and feelings of worthlessness. Only one of the placebo patients similarly improved.

Summary

In summary, the best way to keep your heart, brain, joints, skin, and mood healthy and happy is to avoid unhealthy fats and to emphasize healthy fats such as omega fatty acids found in fish, nuts, seeds, green leafy vegetables, sea vegetables, and oils from vegetables or seeds. Unhealthy fats include trans fats from deep-fried foods, hydrogenated fats found in hard margarines and baked goods, and saturated fats found in butter, high-fat dairy foods, and meats.

Main Points in Chapter 8

- The brain relies on the proper ratio of omega-3 to omega-6 fatty acids for many of its functions, especially mood control and neurotransmitter production.
- Omega-3 fatty acids are found in fish, flaxseeds, walnuts, canola, soy, and green leafy vegetables.
- Trans fats should be avoided.

9

Two Weeks
of Feel-Good
Plan I Meals

Here are fourteen days of menus for each of the plans in the Feel-Good Diet. Once you follow our examples, you will quickly learn the pattern of how the meals and serotonin snacks work. This way you can adapt the program to fit your own schedule and food preferences. Dishes in italics are recipes that can be found in Chapter 14.

Feel-Good Diet Plan I Meals

We offer three types of meal plans based on your particular needs. To determine which is right for you, please refer to the discussion in Chapter 7.

DAY 1

Plan A	Plan B	Plan C

Before Breakfast

Super pH Water	Super pH Water	Super pH Water

Breakfast

½ cup *Fried Potatoes*	½ cup *Fried Potatoes*	½ cup *Fried Potatoes*
2 eggs	2 eggs	4 eggs
		1 slice whole wheat toast with 1 teaspoon healthy margarine

Midmorning Serotonin-Boosting Snack

¾ cup fresh blueberries with 2 tablespoons Coffee-Mate Carb Select fat-free coffee creamer	¾ cup fresh blueberries with 2 tablespoons Coffee-Mate Carb Select fat-free coffee creamer	¾ cup fresh blueberries with 2 tablespoons Coffee-Mate Carb Select fat-free coffee creamer

Before Lunch

Super pH Water	Super pH Water	Super pH Water

Lunch

Classic Chicken Salad with 2 ounces chicken and ½ cup fat-free croutons	*Classic Chicken Salad* with 4 ounces chicken and ½ cup fat-free croutons	*Classic Chicken Salad* with 4 ounces chicken and ½ cup fat-free croutons
Vinaigrette dressing	Vinaigrette dressing	Vinaigrette dressing

Afternoon Serotonin-Boosting Snack

20 Baked! Tostitos chips	20 Baked! Tostitos chips	20 Baked! Tostitos chips

Plan A	Plan B	Plan C
Before Dinner		
Super pH Water	Super pH Water	Super pH Water
Dinner		
2 ounces *Grilled Salmon Fillet*	4 ounces *Grilled Salmon Fillet*	4 ounces *Grilled Salmon Fillet*
Grilled Vegetables	*Grilled Vegetables*	*Grilled Vegetables*
⅓ cup *Quick Brown Rice Pilaf*	⅓ cup *Quick Brown Rice Pilaf*	⅓ cup *Quick Brown Rice Pilaf*
Evening Serotonin-Boosting Snack		
3 cups 94 percent fat-free popcorn	3 cups 94 percent fat-free popcorn	3 cups 94 percent fat-free popcorn

DAY 2

Plan A	Plan B	Plan C
Before Breakfast		
Super pH Water	Super pH Water	Super pH Water
Breakfast		
2 *Oat and Wheat Germ Pancakes*	2 *Oat and Wheat Germ Pancakes*	4 *Oat and Wheat Germ Pancakes*
1 teaspoon healthy margarine	1 teaspoon healthy margarine	2 teaspoons healthy margarine
Sugar-free syrup	Sugar-free syrup	Sugar-free syrup
2 ounces smoked turkey sausage	2 ounces smoked turkey sausage	4 ounces smoked turkey sausage
Midmorning Serotonin-Boosting Snack		
⅓ medium cantaloupe	⅓ medium cantaloupe	⅓ medium cantaloupe

Plan A	Plan B	Plan C

Before Lunch

Super pH Water	Super pH Water	Super pH Water

Lunch

2 ounces cooked shrimp and no-sugar-added cocktail sauce	4 ounces cooked shrimp and no-sugar-added cocktail sauce	4 ounces cooked shrimp and no-sugar-added cocktail sauce
Raw vegetables	Raw vegetables	Raw vegetables
5 Triscuits	5 Triscuits	5 Triscuits

Afternoon Serotonin-Boosting Snack

1 cup light cranberry juice cocktail	1 cup light cranberry juice cocktail	1 cup light cranberry juice cocktail

Before Dinner

Super pH Water	Super pH Water	Super pH Water

Dinner

French Onion Soup	*French Onion Soup*	*French Onion Soup*
2 ounces *Southwest London Broil*	4 ounces *Southwest London Broil*	4 ounces *Southwest London Broil*
Grilled Vegetables	*Grilled Vegetables*	*Grilled Vegetables*

Evening Serotonin-Boosting Snack

1½ cups fresh strawberries with 2 tablespoons fat-free whipped topping	1½ cups fresh strawberries with 2 tablespoons fat-free whipped topping	1½ cups fresh strawberries with 2 tablespoons fat-free whipped topping

DAY 3

Plan A	Plan B	Plan C

Before Breakfast

Super pH Water

Super pH Water

Super pH Water

Breakfast

Plan A	Plan B	Plan C
1 serving *Vanilla Cream Instant Oatmeal*	1 serving *Vanilla Cream Instant Oatmeal*	2 servings *Vanilla Cream Instant Oatmeal*
¼ cup nonfat or 1 percent milk	¼ cup nonfat or 1 percent milk	½ cup nonfat or 1 percent milk
1 egg	1 egg	2 eggs

Midmorning Serotonin-Boosting Snack

Plan A	Plan B	Plan C
1 cup fresh papaya	1 cup fresh papaya	1 cup fresh papaya

Before Lunch

Plan A	Plan B	Plan C
Super pH Water	Super pH Water	Super pH Water

Lunch

Plan A	Plan B	Plan C
1 serving *Taco Salad*	2 servings *Taco Salad*	2 servings *Taco Salad*

Afternoon Serotonin-Boosting Snack

Plan A	Plan B	Plan C
¾ ounce pretzels	¾ ounce pretzels	¾ ounce pretzels

Before Dinner

Plan A	Plan B	Plan C
Super pH Water	Super pH Water	Super pH Water

Dinner

Plan A	Plan B	Plan C
1 serving *Ginger Beef*	2 servings *Ginger Beef*	2 servings *Ginger Beef*
⅓ cup steamed rice	⅓ cup steamed rice	⅓ cup steamed rice

Plan A	Plan B	Plan C

Evening Serotonin-Boosting Snack

Plan A	Plan B	Plan C
¼-inch-thick slice pound cake with ½ cup fresh raspberries	¼-inch-thick slice pound cake with ½ cup fresh raspberries	¼-inch-thick slice pound cake with ½ cup fresh raspberries

DAY 4

Plan A	Plan B	Plan C

Before Breakfast

Plan A	Plan B	Plan C
Super pH Water	Super pH Water	Super pH Water

Breakfast

Plan A	Plan B	Plan C
Veggie Omelet (2 eggs)	*Veggie Omelet* (2 eggs)	*Veggie Omelet* (4 eggs)
1 piece of toast with 1 teaspoon healthy margarine	1 piece of toast with 1 teaspoon healthy margarine	2 pieces of toast with 1 teaspoon healthy margarine

Midmorning Serotonin-Boosting Snack

Plan A	Plan B	Plan C
1 cup light cranberry juice cocktail	1 cup light cranberry juice cocktail	1 cup light cranberry juice cocktail

Before Lunch

Plan A	Plan B	Plan C
Super pH Water	Super pH Water	Super pH Water

Lunch

Plan A	Plan B	Plan C
1 *Tuna Melt*	1 *Tuna Melt*	1 *Tuna Melt*
1 serving *Tomato Bisque*	1 serving *Tomato Bisque*	1 serving *Tomato Bisque*
	½ cup fat-free cottage cheese	½ cup fat-free cottage cheese

Plan A	**Plan B**	**Plan C**

Afternoon Serotonin-Boosting Snack

7 Baked! Lay's Potato Crisps	7 Baked! Lay's Potato Crisps	7 Baked! Lay's Potato Crisps

Before Dinner

Super pH Water	Super pH Water	Super pH Water

Dinner

1 *Chicken or Beef Fajita*	1 *Chicken or Beef Fajita*	1 *Chicken or Beef Fajita*
Fat-free sour cream	Fat-free sour cream	Fat-free sour cream
Salsa	Salsa	Salsa
	⅔ cup fat-free refried beans	⅔ cup fat-free refried beans

Evening Serotonin-Boosting Snack

⅓ cup mandarin orange sections in sugar-free gelatin	⅓ cup mandarin orange sections in sugar-free gelatin	⅓ cup mandarin orange sections in sugar-free gelatin

DAY 5

Plan A	**Plan B**	**Plan C**

Before Breakfast

Super pH Water	Super pH Water	Super pH Water

Breakfast

1 serving ready-to-eat cereal (see Chapter 7 for portions)	1 serving ready-to-eat cereal (see Chapter 7 for portions)	2 servings ready-to-eat cereal (see Chapter 7 for portions)

Plan A	Plan B	Plan C

Breakfast (cont.)

Plan A	Plan B	Plan C
2 tablespoons fresh blueberries	2 tablespoons fresh blueberries	¼ cup fresh blueberries
2 tablespoons slivered almonds	2 tablespoons slivered almonds	¼ cup slivered almonds
1 cup nonfat or 1 percent milk	1 cup nonfat or 1 percent milk	2 cups nonfat or 1 percent milk

Midmorning Serotonin-Boosting Snack

Plan A	Plan B	Plan C
½ cup orange juice	½ cup orange juice	½ cup orange juice

Before Lunch

Plan A	Plan B	Plan C
Super pH Water	Super pH Water	Super pH Water

Lunch

Plan A	Plan B	Plan C
1 cup *Greek Salad*	1 cup *Greek Salad*	1 cup *Greek Salad*
1 whole wheat roll with 1 teaspoon healthy margarine	1 whole wheat roll with 1 teaspoon healthy margarine	1 whole wheat roll with 1 teaspoon healthy margarine
1 serving *Easy Beef and Bean Soup*	2 servings *Easy Beef and Bean Soup*	2 servings *Easy Beef and Bean Soup*

Afternoon Serotonin-Boosting Snack

Plan A	Plan B	Plan C
5 reduced-fat woven wheat crackers	5 reduced-fat woven wheat crackers	5 reduced-fat woven wheat crackers

Before Dinner

Plan A	Plan B	Plan C
Super pH Water	Super pH Water	Super pH Water

Plan A	Plan B	Plan C
Dinner		
1 serving thin-crust pizza (see Fast-Food List, Chapter 7)	1 serving thin-crust pizza (see Fast-Food List, Chapter 7)	1 serving thin-crust pizza (see Fast-Food List, Chapter 7)
Mixed green salad	Mixed green salad	Mixed green salad
		½ cup cottage cheese
Nonfat Italian dressing	Nonfat Italian dressing	Nonfat Italian dressing

Evening Serotonin-Boosting Snack

Plan A	Plan B	Plan C
1 serving *Raisins Dipped in Chocolate*	1 serving *Raisins Dipped in Chocolate*	1 serving *Raisins Dipped in Chocolate*

Day 6

Plan A	Plan B	Plan C
Before Breakfast		
Super pH Water	Super pH Water	Super pH Water
Breakfast		
Make-Ahead Egg Custard	*Make-Ahead Egg Custard*	*Make-Ahead Egg Custard* (double serving)
½ grapefruit	½ grapefruit	Whole grapefruit
		20-ounce sugar-free, nonfat latte

Plan A	Plan B	Plan C

Midmorning Serotonin-Boosting Snack

1 cup light grape juice	1 cup light grape juice	1 cup light grape juice

Before Lunch

Super pH Water	Super pH Water	Super pH Water

Lunch

1 ounce 98 percent fat-free ham and 1 ounce light Jarlsberg on rye	3 ounces 98 percent fat-free ham and 1 ounce light Jarlsberg on rye	3 ounces 98 percent fat-free ham and 1 ounce light Jarlsberg on rye
Mixed green salad with fat-free ranch dressing	Mixed green salad with fat-free ranch dressing	Mixed green salad with fat-free ranch dressing

Afternoon Serotonin-Boosting Snack

2 teaspoons raisins with 2 tablespoons fat-free granola	2 teaspoons raisins with 2 tablespoons fat-free granola	2 teaspoons raisins with 2 tablespoons fat-free granola

Before Dinner

Super pH Water	Super pH Water	Super pH Water

Dinner

Asian Shrimp and Vegetables with 2 ounces shrimp and ½ cup angel hair pasta	*Asian Shrimp and Vegetables* with 4 ounces shrimp and ½ cup angel hair pasta	*Asian Shrimp and Vegetables* with 4 ounces shrimp and ½ cup angel hair pasta

Evening Serotonin-Boosting Snack

1½ slices pineapple in juice with 2 tablespoons fat-free whipped topping	1½ slices pineapple in juice with 2 tablespoons fat-free whipped topping	1½ slices pineapple in juice with 2 tablespoons fat-free whipped topping

DAY 7

Plan A	Plan B	Plan C

Before Breakfast

Plan A	Plan B	Plan C
Super pH Water	Super pH Water	Super pH Water

Breakfast

Plan A	Plan B	Plan C
Ham and Cheese Omelet (2 eggs)	*Ham and Cheese Omelet* (2 eggs)	*Ham and Cheese Omelet* (4 eggs)
1 slice of toast with 1 teaspoon healthy margarine	1 slice of toast with 1 teaspoon healthy margarine	2 slices of toast with 2 teaspoons healthy margarine

Midmorning Serotonin-Boosting Snack

Plan A	Plan B	Plan C
Banana half	Banana half	Banana half

Before Lunch

Plan A	Plan B	Plan C
Super pH Water	Super pH Water	Super pH Water

Lunch

Plan A	Plan B	Plan C
Deli Turkey Wrap with 2 ounces turkey	*Deli Turkey Wrap* with 4 ounces turkey	*Deli Turkey Wrap* with 4 ounces turkey
Mixed green salad	Mixed green salad	Mixed green salad
Fat-free ranch dressing	Fat-free ranch dressing	Fat-free ranch dressing

Afternoon Serotonin-Boosting Snack

Plan A	Plan B	Plan C
1 serving *Mocha Crisp*	1 serving *Mocha Crisp*	1 serving *Mocha Crisp*

Before Dinner

Plan A	Plan B	Plan C
Super pH Water	Super pH Water	Super pH Water

Plan A	Plan B	Plan C
Dinner		
1 serving of *Chicken and Kashi Casserole* with 2 ounces chicken	1 serving of *Chicken and Kashi Casserole* with 4 ounces chicken	1 serving of *Chicken and Kashi Casserole* with 4 ounces chicken
Steamed broccoli	Steamed broccoli	Steamed broccoli
Evening Serotonin-Boosting Snack		
½ cup fruit cocktail in juice with 2 tablespoons fat-free whipped topping	½ cup fruit cocktail in juice with 2 tablespoons fat-free whipped topping	½ cup fruit cocktail in juice with 2 tablespoons fat-free whipped topping

DAY 8

Plan A	Plan B	Plan C
Before Breakfast		
Super pH Water	Super pH Water	Super pH Water
Breakfast		
1 *Breakfast Burrito*	1 *Breakfast Burrito*	2 *Breakfast Burritos*
Midmorning Serotonin-Boosting Snack		
⅛ medium honeydew	⅛ medium honeydew	⅛ medium honeydew
Before Lunch		
Super pH Water	Super pH Water	Super pH Water
Lunch		
Crab salad with 2 ounces crab and fat-free Thousand Island dressing	Crab salad with 4 ounces crab and fat-free Thousand Island dressing	Crab salad with 4 ounces crab and fat-free Thousand Island dressing

Plan A	Plan B	Plan C
1 slice bread with dipping oil	1 slice bread with dipping oil	1 slice bread with dipping oil

Afternoon Serotonin-Boosting Snack

1 *S'more Serotonin Snack*	1 *S'more Serotonin Snack*	1 *S'more Serotonin Snack*

Before Dinner

Super pH Water	Super pH Water	Super pH Water

Dinner

2 ounces *Chicken in Wine*	4 ounces *Chicken in Wine*	4 ounces *Chicken in Wine*
⅓ cup *Quick Brown Rice Pilaf*	⅓ cup *Quick Brown Rice Pilaf*	⅓ cup *Quick Brown Rice Pilaf*
Sautéed Vegetables	*Sautéed Vegetables*	*Sautéed Vegetables*

Evening Serotonin-Boosting Snack

17 frozen grapes	17 frozen grapes	17 frozen grapes

DAY 9

Plan A	Plan B	Plan C

Before Breakfast

Super pH Water	Super pH Water	Super pH Water

Breakfast

Subway Breakfast Wrap (cheese)	Subway Breakfast Wrap (cheese)	Subway Breakfast Wrap (Western with cheese)

Midmorning Serotonin-Boosting Snack

⅛ medium honeydew	⅛ medium honeydew	⅛ medium honeydew

Plan A	Plan B	Plan C

Before Lunch

Super pH Water	Super pH Water	Super pH Water

Lunch

Chinese Cabbage Salad with 2 ounces cooked chicken breast	*Chinese Cabbage Salad* with 4 ounces cooked chicken breast	*Chinese Cabbage Salad* with 4 ounces cooked chicken breast
½ cup mandarin oranges in juice	½ cup mandarin oranges in juice	½ cup mandarin oranges in juice

Afternoon Serotonin-Boosting Snack

1 rice cake	1 rice cake	1 rice cake

Before Dinner

Super pH Water	Super pH Water	Super pH Water

Dinner

½ cup pasta with 2 ounces turkey Italian sausage and ready-to-serve pasta sauce with no sugar added	½ cup pasta with 4 ounces turkey Italian sausage and ready-to-serve pasta sauce with no sugar added	½ cup pasta with 4 ounces turkey Italian sausage and ready-to-serve pasta sauce with no sugar added
Romaine lettuce with fat-free Caesar dressing	Romaine lettuce with fat-free Caesar dressing	Romaine lettuce with fat-free Caesar dressing

Evening Serotonin-Boosting Snack

1 cup fresh strawberries with *Chocolate "Cheer-You-Up" Sauce*	1 cup fresh strawberries with *Chocolate "Cheer-You-Up" Sauce*	1 cup fresh strawberries with *Chocolate "Cheer-You-Up" Sauce*

DAY 10

Plan A	Plan B	Plan C

Before Breakfast

Plan A	Plan B	Plan C
Super pH Water	Super pH Water	Super pH Water

Breakfast

Plan A	Plan B	Plan C
1 poached egg	1 poached egg	2 poached eggs
1 ounce 97 percent fat-free ham or Canadian bacon	1 ounce 97 percent fat-free ham or Canadian bacon	2 ounces 97 percent fat-free ham or Canadian bacon
½ English muffin	½ English muffin	1 English muffin

Midmorning Serotonin-Boosting Snack

Plan A	Plan B	Plan C
¾ cup fresh blueberries with 2 tablespoons Coffee-Mate Carb Select fat-free coffee creamer	¾ cup fresh blueberries with 2 tablespoons Coffee-Mate Carb Select fat-free coffee creamer	¾ cup fresh blueberries with 2 tablespoons Coffee-Mate Carb Select fat-free coffee creamer

Before Lunch

Plan A	Plan B	Plan C
Super pH Water	Super pH Water	Super pH Water

Lunch

Plan A	Plan B	Plan C
2 ounces grilled chicken	4 ounces grilled chicken	4 ounces grilled chicken
Lettuce, tomato, and other veggies as desired	Lettuce, tomato, and other veggies as desired	Lettuce, tomato, and other veggies as desired
1 La Tortilla Factory low-carb tortilla	1 La Tortilla Factory low-carb tortilla	1 La Tortilla Factory low-carb tortilla

Plan A	Plan B	Plan C
Afternoon Serotonin-Boosting Snack		
20 Baked! Tostitos chips	20 Baked! Tostitos chips	20 Baked! Tostitos chips
Before Dinner		
Super pH Water	Super pH Water	Super pH Water
Dinner		
2 ounces *Grilled Pork Loin Steaks with Rosemary*	4 ounces *Grilled Pork Loin Steaks with Rosemary*	4 ounces *Grilled Pork Loin Steaks with Rosemary*
Seasoned green beans	Seasoned green beans	Seasoned green beans
1 serving *Garlic Mashed Potatoes*	1 serving *Garlic Mashed Potatoes*	1 serving *Garlic Mashed Potatoes*
Evening Serotonin-Boosting Snack		
1 cup frozen raspberries in sugar-free gelatin	1 cup frozen raspberries in sugar-free gelatin	1 cup frozen raspberries in sugar-free gelatin

DAY 11

Plan A	Plan B	Plan C
Before Breakfast		
Super pH Water	Super pH Water	Super pH Water
Breakfast		
1 whole wheat frozen waffle	1 whole wheat frozen waffle	2 whole wheat frozen waffles
1 teaspoon healthy margarine	1 teaspoon healthy margarine	2 teaspoons healthy margarine

Plan A	Plan B	Plan C
Sugar-free syrup	Sugar-free syrup	Sugar-free syrup
2 ounces 97 percent fat-free ham	2 ounces 97 percent fat-free ham	4 ounces 97 percent fat-free ham

Midmorning Serotonin-Boosting Snack

⅓ medium cantaloupe	⅓ medium cantaloupe	⅓ medium cantaloupe

Before Lunch

Super pH Water	Super pH Water	Super pH Water

Lunch

2 ounces smoked salmon	2 ounces smoked salmon	2 ounces smoked salmon
Vegetable juice	Vegetable juice	Vegetable juice
5 Triscuits	5 Triscuits	5 Triscuits
	½ cup nonfat cottage cheese	½ cup nonfat cottage cheese

Afternoon Serotonin-Boosting Snack

1 slice French bread with dipping oil	1 slice French bread with dipping oil	1 slice French bread with dipping oil

Before Dinner

Super pH Water	Super pH Water	Super pH Water

Dinner

Any variety of Lean Cuisine Spa Cuisine frozen entrées	Any variety of Lean Cuisine Spa Cuisine frozen entrées	Any variety of Lean Cuisine Spa Cuisine frozen entrées
	1 cup nonfat or 1 percent milk	1 cup nonfat or 1 percent milk
	10 raw almonds	10 raw almonds

Plan A	Plan B	Plan C

Evening Serotonin-Boosting Snack

Plan A	Plan B	Plan C
Sliced banana half with 2 tablespoons fat-free whipped topping	Sliced banana half with 2 tablespoons fat-free whipped topping	Sliced banana half with 2 tablespoons fat-free whipped topping

DAY 12

Plan A	Plan B	Plan C

Before Breakfast

Plan A	Plan B	Plan C
Super pH Water	Super pH Water	Super pH Water

Breakfast

Plan A	Plan B	Plan C
20-ounce latte (fat free and sugar free)	20-ounce latte (fat free and sugar free)	20-ounce latte (fat free and sugar free)
1 slice whole-grain toast with cinnamon and sweetener	1 slice whole-grain toast with cinnamon and sweetener	2 slices whole-grain toast with 4 tablespoons peanut butter

Midmorning Serotonin-Boosting Snack

Plan A	Plan B	Plan C
½ cup oatmeal with sweetener (no milk)	½ cup oatmeal with sweetener (no milk)	½ cup oatmeal with sweetener (no milk)

Before Lunch

Plan A	Plan B	Plan C
Super pH Water	Super pH Water	Super pH Water

Lunch

Plan A	Plan B	Plan C
1 cup lentil, split pea, or black bean soup	2 cups lentil, split pea, or black bean soup	2 cups lentil, split pea, or black bean soup

Plan A	Plan B	Plan C
1 slice whole-grain bread with 1 teaspoon healthy margarine	1 slice whole-grain bread with 1 teaspoon healthy margarine	1 slice whole-grain bread with 1 teaspoon healthy margarine
Mixed green salad with fat-free dressing	Mixed green salad with fat-free dressing	Mixed green salad with fat-free dressing

Afternoon Serotonin-Boosting Snack

¾ ounce pretzels	¾ ounce pretzels	¾ ounce pretzels

Before Dinner

Super pH Water	Super pH Water	Super pH Water

Dinner

2 *Asian Lettuce Wraps*	4 *Asian Lettuce Wraps*	4 *Asian Lettuce Wraps*
Egg Drop Soup	*Egg Drop Soup*	*Egg Drop Soup*
1 fortune cookie	1 fortune cookie	1 fortune cookie

Evening Serotonin-Boosting Snack

¼-inch-thick slice pound cake with ½ cup sliced strawberries	¼-inch-thick slice pound cake with ½ cup sliced strawberries	¼-inch-thick slice pound cake with ½ cup sliced strawberries

DAY 13

Plan A	Plan B	Plan C
Before Breakfast		
Super pH Water	Super pH Water	Super pH Water

Plan A	Plan B	Plan C
Breakfast		
One McDonald's Egg McMuffin minus ½ of English muffin	One McDonald's Egg McMuffin minus ½ of English muffin	One McDonald's Egg McMuffin
		McDonald's scrambled eggs
Midmorning Serotonin-Boosting Snack		
½ cup orange juice	½ cup orange juice	½ cup orange juice
Before Lunch		
Super pH Water	Super pH Water	Super pH Water
Lunch		
Sandwich made from 2 slices light bread and 2 ounces low-fat deli meat	Sandwich made from 2 slices light bread and 3 ounces low-fat deli meat and 1 ounce reduced-fat cheese	Sandwich made from 2 slices light bread and 3 ounces low-fat deli meat and 1 ounce reduced-fat cheese
Fat-free mayonnaise, mustard	Fat-free mayonnaise, mustard	Fat-free mayonnaise, mustard
Lettuce, pickles, and tomato	Lettuce, pickles, and tomato	Lettuce, pickles, and tomato
Celery and carrot sticks	Celery and carrot sticks	Celery and carrot sticks
Afternoon Serotonin-Boosting Snack		
1½ cups fresh watermelon	1½ cups fresh watermelon	1½ cups fresh watermelon
Before Dinner		
Super pH Water	Super pH Water	Super pH Water

Plan A	Plan B	Plan C
Dinner		
2 ounces grilled or broiled sirloin steak	4 ounces grilled or broiled sirloin steak	4 ounces grilled or broiled sirloin steak
Small baked potato with healthy margarine and/or fat-free sour cream	Small baked potato with healthy margarine and/or fat-free sour cream	Small baked potato with healthy margarine and/or fat-free sour cream
Steamed mixed vegetables	Steamed mixed vegetables	Steamed mixed vegetables
Mixed green salad with fat-free vinaigrette dressing	Mixed green salad with fat-free vinaigrette dressing	Mixed green salad with fat-free vinaigrette dressing

Evening Serotonin-Boosting Snack

Plan A	Plan B	Plan C
3 cups 94 percent fat-free popcorn	3 cups 94 percent fat-free popcorn	3 cups 94 percent fat-free popcorn

DAY 14

Plan A	Plan B	Plan C
Before Breakfast		
Super pH Water	Super pH Water	Super pH Water
Breakfast		
One slice *French Toast* with sugar-free syrup	One slice *French Toast* with sugar-free syrup	Two slices *French Toast* with sugar-free syrup
1 Boca Breakfast patty	1 Boca Breakfast patty	2 Boca Breakfast patties

Midmorning Serotonin-Boosting Snack

Plan A	Plan B	Plan C
½ cup orange juice	½ cup orange juice	½ cup orange juice

Plan A	Plan B	Plan C

Before Lunch

Super pH Water	Super pH Water	Super pH Water

Lunch

¾ cup 99 percent fat-free chili	1½ cups 99 percent fat-free chili	1½ cups 99 percent fat-free chili
2-inch-square slice of cornbread from fat-free mix with 1 teaspoon healthy margarine	2-inch-square slice of cornbread from fat-free mix with 1 teaspoon healthy margarine	2-inch-square slice of cornbread from fat-free mix with 1 teaspoon healthy margarine

Afternoon Serotonin-Boosting Snack

7 Baked! Lay's Potato Crisps	7 Baked! Lay's Potato Crisps	7 Baked! Lay's Potato Crisps

Before Dinner

Super pH Water	Super pH Water	Super pH Water

Dinner

Easy Stuffed Peppers	*Easy Stuffed Peppers*	*Easy Stuffed Peppers*
Mixed green salad with nonfat Italian dressing	Mixed green salad with nonfat Italian dressing	Mixed green salad with nonfat Italian dressing
	1 hard-boiled egg	1 hard-boiled egg
	2 tablespoons raw sunflower seeds	2 tablespoons raw sunflower seeds

Evening Serotonin-Boosting Snack

1 ounce dark 70 percent cocoa chocolate bar	1 ounce dark 70 percent cocoa chocolate bar	1 ounce dark 70 percent cocoa chocolate bar

10

Using Supplements to Help Boost Neurotransmitters

The two neurotransmitters that have the most effect on your mood, appetite, cravings, and sex drive are serotonin and dopamine. As explained in Chapter 4, calorie restrictions and the stress of dieting lower the amounts of these you normally make. Research at Oxford has found that women who are on a low-calorie diet even for just three weeks have lowered their tryptophan levels and have also damaged the system that turns tryptophan into serotonin.

Recall that tryptophan needs the help of insulin and carbohydrates in order to enter the brain to be made into serotonin. If, however, insulin levels are raised too much, it can lead to insulin resistance. Chapter 6 discusses this insulin-serotonin dilemma in detail. Our Feel-Good Diet Plan I outlines a way of raising your serotonin with food while still controlling insulin, but it may not be enough for your individual needs. As discussed in Chapter 4, there are many causes of neurotransmitter deficiencies. Depending on the causes and how severely low your levels are, you may need to consider using special supplements to get them back in balance. Research also shows that the more overweight you are, the less serotonin your body naturally makes. Our clinical experience with the women we see every day agrees with that data. We find that raising serotonin levels with supplements as described in Plan II is very successful for helping significantly overweight clients control their appetite and cravings.

Neurotransmitter Precursor Supplements Are Recommended When:

- You find it difficult or inconvenient to fit in all of your daily serotonin-boosting snacks.
- You get extremely tired or shaky twenty minutes to two hours after having a serotonin-boosting snack.
- You find that you still have trouble with controlling cravings.
- You find that you need to make a lot more serotonin. This often occurs when you are under stress. Completing the Serotonin Restore Score questionnaire in Chapter 13 will help you determine your current levels of serotonin and how much more you need to replace.

Plan II (Chapter 13) is a modification of Plan I and can raise serotonin and dopamine levels even more. Supplements are used instead of, or in addition to, serotonin-boosting snacks.

Raising Serotonin Levels with Supplements

As we have discussed, the amino acid tryptophan is the starting point for making serotonin. Tryptophan is no longer available as an over-the-counter supplement in the United States. It was banned in 1990 because of an outbreak of a serious blood disorder called *eosinophilia myalgia.* A contaminant in the manufacturing process of just one batch, not tryptophan itself, is thought to have caused the disorder. Nonetheless, it is still available only by prescription. Fortunately, a derivative of tryptophan, called 5-hydroxytryptophan (5-HTP), is widely available as a dietary supplement. It actually has an advantage over tryptophan in that it is one step closer to converting to serotonin. Also, 5-HTP diffuses easily into the brain and does not need the help of carbohydrates and insulin in order to get in. For these reasons, 5-HTP produces higher and more effective levels of serotonin.

The 5-HTP supplement is not commercially made from tryptophan but is extracted from the seeds of the *Griffonia simplicifolia* plant. The extract has a huge variance in the amount of 5-HTP it contains. It can range in purity from 40 to 99.8 percent. The quality and purity of dietary supplements are not government regulated, so 5-HTP capsules sold over the counter vary considerably in purity and actual dosage. Recently, dietary supplement companies have united to form quality-assurance organizations. The National Nutritional Foods Association (NNFA) is the primary organization in this regard. Products meeting their quality standards are given special certifications that are usually printed on product labels. The 5-HTP supplement is commonly sold in capsules containing 25, 50, or 100 milligrams of the *Griffonia simplicifolia* seed extract. It is important to check the ingredient label to ensure that you are getting the highest level of active 5-HTP in your product.

Studies using 5-HTP in amounts of 750 to 900 milligrams per day have been shown to reduce appetite even when the people tested were not following any particular diet. They found that 5-HTP was most effective when the dose was divided and taken two or three times per day. We have used similar doses in our clinic to help clients stick to their diets.

Some people experience nausea or diarrhea while ingesting 5-HTP in capsule form. The digestive system contains 90 percent of the body's serotonin receptors. When large amounts of 5-HTP are ingested, the burst of serotonin produced is attracted to these receptors in the walls of the intestine. High levels of intestinal serotonin can lead to nausea, abdominal cramping, and diarrhea. While some people can adjust to it, many find it necessary to skip or lower their doses in order to alleviate these problems. Lowered doses may not be as effective in decreasing appetite or controlling cravings.

Food can interfere with the absorption of 5-HTP into the bloodstream. To get the best response, you should avoid eating anything for about half an hour after taking 5-HTP capsules orally.

Other side effects of 5-HTP include headaches and drowsiness. Drowsiness occurs because excess serotonin converts to the sleep hormone melatonin.

Several studies support the idea of combining serotonin precursors with antidepressant therapy. Serotonin-enhancing antidepressants (called SSRIs), such as Prozac, Zoloft, Paxil, Lexapro, and Effexor, may work better when more serotonin is produced in the neurons. A rare but serious condition, the serotonin syndrome, can result if you flood your body with too much serotonin. The signs and symptoms of serotonin syndrome include high body temperature, erratic blood pressure, fast breathing, flushing, skin clamminess, and mental confusion. While combining 5-HTP and SSRIs theoretically could cause this condition, no actual occurrences have been reported. In any case, if you are on antidepressants, we advise that you talk to your physician before starting 5-HTP supplements.

Serotonin Needs a Partner—Dopamine

Another problem many people experience after using large doses of 5-HTP is waking up in the morning feeling groggy or hazy. Some describe feeling as though they have a "hangover" with nausea, upset stomach, and a pounding headache. Our clinical experience helped us eliminate these annoying serotonin side effects by counterbalancing the effects with more dopamine. This was achieved by adding the amino acid tyrosine, the direct precursor to dopamine. Combining 5-HTP with tyrosine produces balanced amounts of both serotonin and dopamine. This successfully eliminates most side effects of excess serotonin.

Dopamine also gets depleted while dieting and during long-term stress. Even though tyrosine is readily available from most protein, the average diet does not contain enough to produce the amounts of dopamine you need under these circumstances. Tyrosine is available as a dietary supplement in 500 milligram capsules. The average dose is 500 to 1,000 milligrams taken twice a day. Because dopamine can be stimulating, people should avoid taking tyrosine in the evening if they notice it keeps them awake at night. Tyrosine is safe to use. According to research, up to 10 grams (10,000 mg) per day have been used in studies to improve responses to highly stressful situations. No adverse affects were reported.

Necessary Vitamin and Mineral Cofactors

The conversion of tryptophan or 5-HTP to serotonin and of tyrosine to dopamine occurs in the brain with the help of their related enzymes. These enzymes need certain vitamins and minerals to function. Serotonin and dopamine production requires vitamin B_6, folic acid, calcium, and magnesium. Converting tyrosine to dopamine also requires copper. It is usually not necessary to supplement copper, as most people get plenty in their diets. Recent research indicates that the trace mineral selenium is also required. Only small amounts of selenium (70 to 200 mcg) should be supplemented daily. Amounts exceeding 550 micrograms a day could be toxic to the brain. Table 10.1 lists the recommended doses of several vitamins and minerals for making neurotransmitters.

TABLE 10.1 Vitamin and Mineral Supplements for Making Neurotransmitters

VITAMIN OR MINERAL	U.S. RECOMMENDED DAILY ALLOWANCE	RECOMMENDED DAILY DOSE FOR MAKING NEUROTRANSMITTERS
Pyridoxine (B$_6$)	2 milligrams	10 to 25 milligrams
Folic acid	200 micrograms	400 to 800 micrograms
Calcium aspartate or calcuim orotate	800 milligrams (any calcium)	500 to 1,000 milligrams calcium aspartate or orotate only
Magnesium aspartate or magnesium orotate	350 milligrams (any magnesium)	500 to 1,000 milligrams magnesium aspartate or orotate only
Copper	1.5 to 3 milligrams	1.5 to 3 milligrams
Zinc	8 to 11 milligrams	15 milligrams

1,000 micrograms = 1 milligram.

Sublingual Neurotransmitter Precursors

Earlier, we discussed why high doses of oral 5-HTP supplements may be needed to relieve low serotonin symptoms. These doses, however, can cause intestinal upset and other side effects. To eliminate these problems, other 5-HTP delivery forms have been tried. The most successful route recently developed is the sublingual one. *Sublingual* just means "under the tongue." These are usually in the form of a lozenge that you dissolve in your mouth. Active ingredients are absorbed directly through the mucous membranes. Bypassing the digestive tract eliminates the nausea and diarrhea problems encountered with oral capsules. Lesser amounts of 5-HTP and tyrosine can be used to make the same effective amounts of neurotransmitters. By clinical experience, we have found sublingual lozenges to be about three to four times more effective than oral capsules and with fewer side effects. Because of these benefits, we expect that sublingual delivery will give you better results than oral capsules.

At our Wellness Workshop clinic, we tested the effectiveness of the sublingual neurotransmitter supplements. Three studies were done and concluded that:

1. Neurotransmitter precursor lozenges safely and effectively increase serotonin and dopamine within one hour.
2. Consistent use of sublingual neurotransmitter supplements will significantly improve symptoms of neurotransmitter deficiencies for most people within four weeks.
3. Improvement in symptoms of neurotransmitter deficiencies using the "active" precursor lozenges was dramatically more effective than in the placebo. For symptoms related to food, mood, and energy, the lozenges with active ingredients were several times more effective than the placebo. The details of these studies appear in Appendix A.

Main Points in Chapter 10

- Brain levels of serotonin and dopamine can be raised by amino acid supplements.
- Optimal benefits in mood, energy, and appetite control are achieved by supporting both serotonin and dopamine production.
- Many side effects and inconveniences of oral dosing of supplements can be eliminated with sublingual delivery of neurotransmitter precursors.

11

Increasing Your Metabolism: How Exercise and Body pH Balance Can Help

Metabolism is the speed at which your body uses up food for energy. It is measured as calories you burn up in a day's time. Body heat is given off as an energy by-product. Because people burn calories or use up their food at different rates, we say they have different rates of metabolism.

What You Need to Know About Metabolism

True or false? "The more overweight you are, the slower your metabolism is."

The answer is false. The truth is that the more overweight you are, the *higher* your metabolism is. This is because metabolism is mostly determined by how much muscle you have. Muscles use up the most amounts of calories of any body system. The more overweight you are, the more muscle you have developed to hold up and carry your body around. You can measure how much muscle you have by doing a body composition measurement. This study tells you how much fat and muscle you actually have. The more fat you carry about on your body frame, the more muscle you automatically make to support the extra weight. For every extra five pounds of fat you put on, you automatically make one pound of muscle. The more muscle you have, the more calories your body uses—hence, the higher your metabolism is. Metabolism studies clearly show that overweight individuals have higher resting metabolic rates and require more calories to sustain their body weight than normal-weight individuals. For example, a person weighing 200 pounds requires about 2,200 calories each day to hold his or her weight steady, while someone weighing 140 pounds needs only 1,540 calories.

The heart muscle also uses a lot of energy as you become more overweight. There are about sixty thousand miles of blood vessels in your body. That's enough miles to circle the earth at the equator. Every extra pound of fat contains two hundred more miles of capillary blood vessels. That means if you are fifty pounds overweight, your body makes ten thousand more miles of blood vessels. Consider the amount of work your heart muscle performs as it pumps blood out to every living cell of your body, sixty to eighty times a minute while you are at rest. Now imagine how many more calories of energy your heart needs when you move about or exercise.

Aging, Stress, Dieting, and Overexercising

There are several things besides your weight that affect your metabolism. Among them are aging, stress, repeated dieting, and overexercising.

Aging

As women age past twenty, metabolism slows down by 1 percent each year. By age thirty, if you continued to eat the same amount of food and do the same amount of exercise that you did at twenty, you would be 10 percent heavier. By age forty, metabolism slows down by 20 percent; by age fifty, it's 30 percent slower. Imagine that in order to weigh the same as you did at age twenty you would need to eat 30 percent fewer calories or exercise 30 percent more. Shifts in metabolism as you age are caused by hormone and neurotransmitter imbalances. These changes favor fat making rather than fat losing.

Stress

Stress shifts hormones and neurotransmitters into survival modes that aim to preserve energy and store fat. Nature intended this to be a short-term strategy. Unfortunately, chronic stress depletes many hormones and blunts neurotransmitter production. As a result, your metabolism slows down.

Repeated Dieting

True or false? "The more weight you lose, the faster your metabolism becomes."

The answer is false. In fact, the more weight you lose, the *slower* your metabolism becomes. Overweight people don't realize how much muscle they really have. Over the course of gaining weight, your body develops more muscles to support your body frame. When you lose fat, you no longer need the extra muscle, and so it atrophies (shrinks). As the amount of your muscle decreases, so does your metabolism.

Most people lose weight without paying attention to maintaining their muscles and accidentally end up slowing down their metabolism. Marilyn's weight-loss story is a classic example of this.

Marilyn H. weighed 180 pounds and wanted to get down to 130 pounds for her daughter's wedding. We evaluated her body composition, measuring the amount of body fat and muscle she had.

Her body profile looked like Figure 11.1. Note that lean body mass includes all the muscles, water, blood, lymph, organs, and bones—anything that is not fat.

Marilyn began dieting her usual way by cutting down calories, and she started losing weight. Seeing the pounds drop away on her bathroom scale every week encouraged her to continue. Finally, one morning six months later, she beamed as her scale proclaimed 130 pounds. Now her size-eight body profile looked like Figure 11.2.

Notice that even though she weighed 130 pounds and lost 33 pounds of fat, she also lost 17 pounds of muscle. Having less muscle, her metabolism was slower than when she weighed 180 pounds.

Marilyn found it difficult to keep her weight steady at her goal of 130 pounds. Even though she wasn't eating nearly the amount of food she had before her diet, she started regaining her weight easily. Her weight climbed back up to 180 pounds over the next three months. Nine months later, she weighed 200 pounds. Now her body profiled looked like Figure 11.3.

FIGURE 11.1 Fat/Lean Body Mass Before Dieting

Fat: 40 percent

Lean body mass: 60 percent

Marilyn started at 180 pounds.
Fat: 180 × 40 percent = 72 pounds
Lean body mass: 180 × 60 percent = 108 pounds

FIGURE 11.2 Fat/Lean Body Mass After Dieting

Fat: 30 percent

Lean body mass: 70 percent

Marilyn got down to 130 pounds—50 pounds lighter! But she also lost 17 pounds of lean body mass.
Fat: 130 × 30 percent = 39 pounds
Lean body mass: 130 × 70 percent = 91 pounds

FIGURE 11.3 Fat/Lean Body Mass After Regaining Weight

Fat: 48 percent

Lean body mass: 52 percent

She *gained* 24 pounds of fat and *lost* 4 pounds of lean body mass (muscle).
Fat: 200 × 48 percent = 96 pounds
Lean body mass: 200 × 52 percent = 104 pounds

By the end of her dieting cycle, Marilyn had gained twenty-four pounds of fat and lost four pounds of muscle.

Marilyn got caught in the yo-yo dieter's trap. Not only did she initially lose weight, she lost valuable muscle. This slowed down her metabolism and made it harder to stay at her goal weight. The aim of successful and long-term weight loss is to lose fat while keeping muscle. Eating adequate amounts of protein while dieting is critical. And exercises aimed at building muscle need to be a vital part of your exercise routine.

Overexercising

Avoid exercising to extremes. Overexercising actually lowers metabolism by burning up muscle for energy. Doing high-intensity cardio workouts longer than forty minutes increases your chances of losing muscle and slowing down your metabolism. Your body stores only twenty minutes of extra glucose as glycogen. Glycogen is stored in the liver and muscles. Normally, it is stored up for energy emergencies. If you burn through your glycogen for energy and exercise too vigorously, your body is forced to burn muscle for its next best source of energy. Most people mistakenly think that you burn a lot of fat calories by doing high-intensity workouts. But recent studies from the Olympic Training Camps clearly show that you do not burn fat while doing high-intensity activities. First you burn available glucose for energy, then glycogen, and then you start burning up your muscles. It takes too long to break down fat into glucose for immediate energy. Burning up muscle is a faster way for your body to get energy.

If exercising makes you hungry, it means that you used up your glucose and glycogen stores. Most likely you started burning up muscle. An important thing to remember is that you don't get hungry when you are burning fat.

Chapter 12 gives you more information about how different types of exercises affect your metabolism.

Calorie and Energy Basics

A lot of people notice they keep gaining five, ten, or fifteen pounds, year after year and are frustrated because they really try not to over-eat or "pig out." A review of how your body uses calories reveals a surprising fact. If you eat an extra fifty calories every day that you don't use up, over one year you will gain five pounds. This may be the two Jolly Rancher hard candies you routinely enjoy during the day, the two Hershey's Kisses that you grab from the office candy dish while rushing by, the little handful of ten M&M's that melt in your mouth, or that one piece of red licorice you snatch from the bin on the way out to lunch. An extra 100 calories a day adds on ten extra pounds a year, while 150 extra calories adds on fifteen more pounds. This simple math shows that eating 200 extra calories a day beyond what you use up adds on twenty more pounds each year.

On the brighter side, if you eliminate these extra calories, you will automatically lose the extra weight over a year's time—even without changing anything else. This is why cutting down on any extra calories makes a big difference over a year's time. Think about where you can cut out some meaningless calories from your daily food routine. Just by changing from cream to 2 percent milk in your daily coffee you can lose nine pounds in a year. You can painlessly lose fifteen pounds just by substituting sugar-free flavorings in your daily latte.

To determine how many calories you can eat each day and get to your goal weight, simply multiply your goal weight by ten. For example, if you want to reach a goal weight of 140 pounds, multiply 140 by ten. This means that you need to limit your maximum daily calories to 1,400 if you want to reach 140 pounds.

In order to maintain your goal weight, multiply it by eleven. Using our previous goal weight example, multiply 140 by eleven. After reaching your goal, you can eat up to 1,540 calories per day and maintain your weight at 140 pounds.

Metabolism Basics

Cells need the sugar glucose to function, just as cars need fuel to run. Eating carbohydrates provides the fastest way for the body to get glucose. Proteins and fats can also be converted to glucose, but the process takes much longer.

Oxygen must also be present in the cells to burn glucose for energy. This is similar to a fire needing oxygen to continue burning. Healthy cells burn calories best in an alkaline environment. The water inside and outside of cells contains electrolytes and minerals that constantly try to keep body fluids alkaline rather than acidic.

As cells burn glucose for fuel, they normally produce waste by-products. These wastes are naturally acidic and need to be neutralized so they will not damage healthy cells. Neutralizers are called buffers. The main buffers in your body are the minerals calcium, magnesium, sodium, and potassium. In order for oxygen and other nutrients to enter the cell and waste products to leave the cell, these four alkalinizing elements must be present in adequate and balanced amounts. Cells with low amounts of these buffers cannot expel toxins or neutralize acids very easily. Cell health suffers. When large amounts of calcium are needed to neutralize excess acids, it may be leached from your bones and teeth. This results in osteoporosis (thinning of the bones), tooth loss, and other degenerative diseases.

Acidic cell wastes are often removed from the blood and deposited in soft tissues, such as joints and muscles. This explains why acidity increases arthritis and fibromyalgia. The more acidic a tissue area becomes, the more cell damage occurs, making the body even more acidic.

Carbon dioxide is by far the most acid-forming substance produced by the body, because carbon dioxide and water are the principal end products from the breakdown of food. Carbonic acid forms when carbon dioxide combines with water in the blood. We easily remove carbonic acid as we breathe out through our lungs. Other kinds of acids are also produced as the body functions. Sulfuric acid is a natural by-product of digesting proteins. Normally, acids are buffered and excreted through the kidneys. Lactic acid buildup occurs during intense muscle activity or from muscle damage. Most likely you have felt the aching effects of too much lactic acid buildup. It's the muscle soreness and cramping you start feeling a day or two after exercising.

All cell functions slow down when acid wastes accumulate. High acidity decreases the oxygen-carrying ability of blood. Low oxygen severely compromises cell functions. Acid buildup increases free radical damage inside the cells and eventually causes cell death. Thus, excess cell acid is thought to be the first step toward premature aging, affecting brain function, heart, skin, hormones, joints, blood vessels, and a host of other age-related phenomena. Also, cancer cells thrive in acid environments.

A constantly acidic environment directly causes weight gain by triggering the hormone condition of insulin resistance. Excess amounts of insulin are produced and increase fat storage. See Chapter 6 for more information about insulin resistance.

Fasting and dieting are acid-producing conditions. Acids trigger a hormone starvation response and signal the body to store fat. To prevent this reaction, it is important to eat at least every five hours during the day. Eating breakfast helps reverse the acidity that normally develops during the night.

In the following section we show you how to regulate your body's acid-alkaline balance while dieting.

How Body pH Affects Metabolism

Body pH reflects the acidity or the alkalinity of the body fluids inside and around cells. A proper pH balance is necessary for cells to work correctly. All regulatory body functions, including breathing, circulation, digestion, hormonal production, and excretion, continuously work to maintain normal pH. An overly acidic condition of the body develops whenever your ability to remove acids is impaired or when your intake of acid-forming elements is excessive.

A pH scale measures how acidic or alkaline a solution is. The scale runs from 0 to 14 with 7 being at the midpoint. A pH number larger than 7 is alkaline, while a pH below 7 is acidic. Distilled water has a pH of 7 and is considered neutral. Vinegar has a pH of 3 and so is an acid. Baking soda's pH of 12 makes it alkaline. The pH of blood is normally slightly alkaline at 7.4. Imbalances of pH affect sleep patterns, energy levels, appetite, food desires, body weight, and mental states. Headaches, body aches, and pains all indicate errors in pH and the body's attempt to correct or compensate. Acidosis, an extended time in the acidic pH state, can result in rheumatoid arthritis, diabetes, lupus, osteoporosis, and cancers.

The types of foods we eat have the most influence in maintaining proper pH levels throughout the body. When food is broken down and metabolized, it leaves certain chemical and metallic residues called "metabolic ash." When combined with body fluids, metabolic ash becomes either acidic or alkaline. Certain foods are "acid forming," whereas others are "alkaline forming." According to modern biochemistry, it is not the organic part of foods that leaves acidic or alkaline residues in the body. The amounts of their inorganic matter such as sulfur, phosphorus, potassium, sodium, magnesium, and calcium determine whether they are acid or alkaline forming.

The general consensus of Western nutritionists is that the healthiest pH balance in the body is achieved by eating 80 percent alkaline-forming foods and 20 percent acid-forming foods. When this four-to-one alkaline-to-acid ratio is maintained, there is strong resistance against disease. People recovering from illnesses are more acidotic. Adjusting their diets to be more alkaline helps them recover faster.

Problems with Acid-Forming Foods

Acid-producing foods reduce cell vitality and function. They also create excess mucus, which congests and blocks oxygen from entering cells. Acidity occurs when you eat an excess of grains, meat, or dairy. The pH also influences metabolism, the rate that you burn fuel for energy. When cells receive adequate amounts of oxygen, very effective energy is produced. When oxygen delivery is restricted, then there is less energy to power the cells and metabolism slows down.

Excessive amounts of protein in any form—animal or vegetable—are debilitating to the body by affecting body acidity. This ultimately leads to chronic diseases such as arthritis, kidney damage, diabetes, cancer, and osteoporosis. Diets that are too acidic also cause decreased mental functioning. Protein is essential to health but should not be consumed in excess. Proteins are the most acid-forming foods because they make the strongest acids—sulfuric and phosphoric acids. Other wastes from digestion of proteins produce the chemical urea in the urine. When exreted, urea drags out alkaline-forming minerals with it.

The following lists are derived from the United States Department of Agriculture's *Composition of Foods*. They divide acid-forming from alkaline-forming foods.

Acid-Forming Foods

Eggs	Grains (most)
Beef	Nuts
Pork	Beans
Chicken	Beer
Fish	Whiskey
Cheese	Sugar

Alkaline-Forming Foods

Salt	Fruits
Miso	Wine

Soy sauce   Coffee

Vegetables   Milk

As a general class, dietary fats are acid forming because they produce acetic acid when metabolized.

Refined foods, simple carbohydrates, regular soft drinks, and most synthetic drugs are acid forming. Alkaline-forming minerals are missing or have been leached out during chemical processing and refining. When you ingest these, your body uses up alkalinizing minerals to neutralize the acid end products. Over time, these mineral buffers are depleted, and an acid shift in the body occurs.

Alkaline-forming foods, such as most vegetables and fruits, are high in sodium, potassium, calcium, and magnesium. These are powerful buffers or acid neutralizers. The acid-forming exceptions are asparagus, cranberries, plums, and prunes.

Complex carbohydrates metabolize more slowly and evenly and therefore don't form organic acids. This improves their acidifying effects.

Even though fruits such as lemons, oranges, grapefruits, tomatoes, and pineapples are acid when you eat them, during the process of digestion they are turned into alkaline substances. This makes them ideal as buffers.

Super pH Water

Removing acid waste products from the cells automatically lets in more oxygen, which means better metabolism. The importance of maintaining proper cell acid-alkaline balance goes beyond just improving your metabolism. Every illness, disease, inflammation, infection, or cancer can be attributed to abnormal amounts of acid retained in the cells.

When your pH is less than ideal, your body works hard to correct it. This leads to fatigue. Drinking a simple, inexpensive, acid-neutralizing drink called Super pH Water is an effective way to neutralize acid cell wastes and increase the amount of oxygen getting into cells. As your cell pH corrects, your overall health improves, boosting your metabolism, energy, and weight loss.

Recipe for a Single Eight-Ounce Serving of Super pH Water

1. Start with eight ounces of chlorine-free, filtered water.
2. Add ½ to 1 teaspoon of organic, raw, unfiltered apple cider vinegar, 5 to 6 percent acidity level. This type of vinegar naturally appears cloudy with sediment at the bottom of the bottle. These particles are called the "mother" and contain the valuable mineral buffers that neutralize acids. If you find the flavor too strong, use less vinegar at first and try increasing it over time.
3. You can add natural sweeteners, as needed, for taste (optional).

Add these important buffering elements to your Super pH Water or take separately as a supplement:

- **Potassium:** at least 200 milligrams potassium aspartate or orotate daily
- **Calcium:** at least 500 milligrams calcium aspartate or orotate daily
- **Magnesium:** 500 to 1,000 milligrams magnesium aspartate or orotate daily

Apple Cider Vinegar

We recommend using up to three tablespoons of apple cider vinegar a day. Always be sure to dilute it in lots of water. Avoid drinking concentrated apple cider vinegar; undiluted vinegar can erode tooth enamel or cause intestinal upset if it is too strong. Drink at least four ounces of plain water after drinking your Super pH Water to avoid damaging your tooth enamel. Alternatively, you could use apple cider vinegar tablets, but they can cause heartburn.

If you cannot tolerate drinking apple cider vinegar, you may substitute the juice of one-half fresh-squeezed lemon per serving. The lemon juice will buffer the pH as vinegar does, but apple cider vinegar works better because it also restores valuable alkalinizing minerals.

The surprising thing about Super pH Water is that although vinegar is acidic (acetic acid), it acts more like a strong alkaline buffer. When acetic acid mixes with a stronger acid, it forms acetate, which is a very strong neutralizer. Unfiltered apple cider vinegar also contains a lot of alkalinizing minerals in the sediment or "mother," which increases its buffering effects.

Apple cider vinegar has other reported benefits including relief of allergies, weight loss, and treatment of acne, high cholesterol, chronic fatigue, candida, acid reflux, sore throats, contact dermatitis, arthritis, gout, and high blood pressure. Scientists have measured ninety different substances in apple cider vinegar, including important minerals, trace elements, vitamins, acetic acid, propionic acid, lactic acid, enzymes, amino acids, as well as roughage in the form of potash and apple pectin.

A 2004 report from Arizona State University published in *Diabetes Care* showed that having an apple cider vinegar drink before eating a carbohydrate meal significantly improved insulin resistance. The investigators went so far as to suggest that vinegar may "possess physiological effects similar to acarbose or metformin," the prescription medications now being used to treat insulin resistance and type 2 diabetes.

Apple cider vinegar has long been touted as a general health tonic. It has been used for centuries as a home remedy and for thousands of years in ancient Asian cultures. Its curative abilities are now attributed to its unique buffering ability. It enables acidic pH levels to become more alkaline, or in the case of an overly alkaline pH, more acidic. Additionally, apple cider vinegar lowers the toxicity of certain compounds by converting them to less toxic compounds.

Potassium, Calcium, and Magnesium

It is important to provide the buffering minerals potassium, calcium, and magnesium every day. They quickly become depleted when cells are acidic. Try to get them through your food (see Tables 11.1 and 11.2), but if that's not possible, you may need to use daily mineral supplements to get enough of them. Use supplement forms that come in a neutral form, such as ascorbate or orotate forms.

TABLE 11.1 Potassium Content of Foods

FOOD	PORTION SIZE	POTASSIUM CONTENT (MG)
Artichoke, cooked	1 medium	425
Asparagus, cooked	½ cup	279
Avocado	½	549 to 742
Banana	1 medium	451
Black-eyed peas, cooked	½ cup	246 to 319
Brussels sprouts, cooked	½ cup	246
Cabbage, raw	1 cup	230
Cantaloupe	½	885
Celery, raw	1 cup	300
Chickpeas, cooked, drained	½ cup	239
Collard greens, cooked	½ cup	214
Corn, cooked	½ cup	204
Dried beans, cooked (black, kidney, or pinto)	½ cup	306 to 398
Figs, dried	5	666
Honeydew melon	¼ medium	875

(continued)

FOOD	PORTION SIZE	POTASSIUM CONTENT (MG)
Kiwifruit	1 medium	252
Lentils, cooked	½ cup	366
Milk	1 cup	370 to 410
Mushrooms, cooked	½ cup	278
Nectarine	1 medium	288
Okra, cooked	½ cup	257
Orange	1 medium	365
Orange juice	½ cup	248
Pear	1 medium	148 to 250
Potato, baked	1 large, no skin	610
Potato, boiled	½ cup	256
Prunes, dried, uncooked	5 large	365
Soybeans, cooked	½ cup	486
Spinach, cooked	½ cup	283 to 420
Spinach, raw	3 to 4 ounces	780
Sweet potato	1 medium	397
Swiss chard, cooked	½ cup	483
Tomato, raw	1 medium	251 to 273
Vegetable juice	11.5 fluid ounces	670 to 800

TABLE 11.2 Foods High in Magnesium

FOOD	SERVING SIZE	MAGNESIUM (MG)
Beans, black	1 cup	120
Broccoli, raw	1 cup	22
Halibut	½ fillet	170
Okra, frozen	1 cup	94
Oysters	3 ounces	49
Peanuts	1 ounce	64
Plantain, raw	1 medium	66

FOOD	SERVING SIZE	MAGNESIUM (MG)
Rockfish	1 fillet	51
Scallops	6 large	55
Seeds, pumpkin and squash	1 ounce (142 seeds)	151
Soy milk	1 cup	47
Spinach, cooked	1 cup	47
Tofu	¼ block	37
Whole-grain cereal, ready to eat	¾ cup	24
Whole-grain cereal, cooked	1 cup	56
Whole wheat bread	1 slice	24

Values were obtained from the USDA Nutrient Database for Standard References, Release 15 for Magnesium, Mg (mg) content of selected foods per common measure. nal.usda.gov/fnic/food comp/data/sr15/wtrank/wt_rank.

Recommended Metabolism-Boosting Plan

Drink your first eight-ounce glass of Super pH Water in the morning soon after you rise and before you eat or drink anything else. This immediately starts neutralizing acid wastes that naturally built up in your body during the night. Remember that even though your body rests while you sleep, vital organs such as your heart, lungs, and brain continue to metabolize nutrients and form acid wastes throughout the night.

Drink an additional eight-ounce glass of Super pH Water about fifteen minutes before your lunch and dinner meals. This helps regulate blood sugar and reduces insulin resistance. These additional doses also increase the speed in which you can lose fat.

Additional pH-Buffering Support

In addition to the eight-ounce glass of Super pH Water before each meal, you may need to drink two more eight-ounce servings (containing one teaspoon to one tablespoon of vinegar in each additional serving) each day if you:

- Are significantly stressed
- Crave or eat a lot of carbohydrates
- Have insulin resistance or diabetes
- Are losing a lot of weight

These conditions significantly increase the amount of acid wastes your body makes. In addition, as you lose weight, hidden toxins and heavy metals are released from fat stores. These need to be buffered as soon as possible so that your body will get rid of them as soon as possible. Some people notice they retain a lot of fluid or feel more tired during the first two weeks of starting the Super pH Water. This is actually a good sign indicating that you are starting to detoxify. Be sure to continue your regimen, trying to maximize your vinegar to the recommended amount. In about seven to ten days you will be rewarded with a drop in your weight and a burst of energy as you start excreting the toxic wastes attached to extra water.

The total amount of apple cider vinegar usually recommended is three tablespoons a day. You may need to add an additional two tablespoons if you are under severe stress, are losing large amounts of weight, strongly crave carbohydrates, or have severe insulin resistance or diabetes. Avoid overdoing the vinegar.

If your Super pH Water tastes too sour, cut back on the amount of vinegar you are using for each serving. If you absolutely cannot tolerate the vinegar, you may substitute concentrated lemon juice, though it is not as effective.

During the first couple of weeks of drinking Super pH Water you may experience some bloating or water retention. This occurs as your body neutralizes previously built-up acids. This eventually goes away as you continue using the Super pH Water.

Water

As babies, we are 90 percent water. As we age our body water content decreases to 70 percent. When we approach complete cellular disorganization (death), we are only 50 percent water. Water helps maintain alkalinity of the body by diluting excess acids that come from cellular metabolism, acidic lifestyles, diets, and even thinking.

The current recommendation for water intake for proper body hydration is six to eight eight-ounce servings of water a day with an additional eight-ounce serving for each twenty-five pounds that you are overweight.

Monitoring pH

Monitoring your internal pH tells you how your whole body is doing. It is an excellent health index. Strips of litmus paper indicate pH values, ideally in two-tenths increments, from moderately strong acid of pH 5.5 to mildly alkaline pH 8.0. This pH test paper tape is widely available at medical supply or health food or supplement stores. The pH paper changes color when it comes in contact with acidic or alkaline substances. A color guide comes with the pH paper. Each color represents a particular pH value. Yellow is acidic, green is neutral to mildly alkaline, and blue is more alkaline.

Stress and Your pH Balance

Saliva pH values are indicators of how your day-to-day emotional stress is affecting your pH balance. Optimal pH for saliva is 6.4 to 6.8. Levels above or below this may cause sharp losses of energy. Readings lower than 6.4 mean that you are more acidic than normal and indicate that you have low amounts of the alkaline mineral buffers calcium, magnesium, sodium, and potassium. If your pH deviates from the norm of 6.4 for a time, sickness and weight problems may result. The greater your range of deviation from 6.4 during a twenty-four-hour period, the more deficient your immune system may be. After eating, saliva pH should rise to 7.8 or higher (turn more alkaline). If not, you don't have enough buffering minerals.

Take the pH Stress Challenge Test

Items needed include litmus pH paper and color guide, small paper cups, and a lemon wedge or lemon juice.

Start by getting a saliva pH baseline as close to your "normal" as possible. For at least two hours, abstain from food and drink, and avoid any other substances you put in your mouth, including tooth-paste, cough drops, chewing gum, breath mints, mouthwash, and cigarette smoke. Use one strip of pH paper (litmus paper). Work up some saliva, and deposit it on the edge of a paper cup. Wet the pH paper against the saliva sample. Compare the color of the wet strip to the pH chart. Write down the pH number corresponding to the color. Then suck on a lemon until the flavor permeates your whole mouth. Dispose of the lemon. Work up some more saliva as you clean off the lemon juice by rubbing your tongue over your teeth and swallowing about four times as you tear off another strip of pH paper. Work up some more saliva and deposit the sample in a clean cup. Again dip the pH strip into the new saliva sample. Compare the color, and write down the corresponding pH number. Now you have two colors and numbers to compare. The first number may be higher than the second, the first number may be lower than the second, or the numbers may be the same.

What Does Your pH Challenge Test Show?

- Yellow is acidic and ranges from pH 5.5 to 6.0.
- Green is less acidic and more neutral. It ranges from pH 6.2 to 7.0.
- Blue is alkaline and ranges from pH 7.2 to 8.0.

Did Your Colors Turn Darker or pH Numbers Get Larger? This means that you have enough alkaline buffers in reserve. Green to blue is the best color change to have. It means you started out being alkaline (green) and got even more alkaline (blue) when you challenged yourself with acidic lemon juice. If your colors went from yellow to green you have some buffers in reserve but not enough when you get stressed. Make sure you are eating fewer acid-forming meat and dairy products (protein) and more alkaline-forming fruits and vegetables.

Did Your Colors Turn Lighter or Your pH Numbers Get Smaller? This means that your baseline levels were alkaline (a good thing) but your body was not able to compensate for the acid challenge. This results in becoming more acidic. Your body is moving toward stress exhaustion. This is seen during times of chronic stress, such as when you are experiencing endless worrying. Saliva pH numbers that go down serve as a warning that your emotional stress could be setting you up for physical health problems. At this point, you are still in control, but you need to make changes to your diet by eating fewer acid-forming meat and dairy products (protein) and more alkaline-forming fruits and vegetables. Also, you need to pay attention to how you are handling stress. Making these changes will help improve your health and energy.

Did Your pH Colors or Numbers Stay the Same? Saliva pH colors or numbers that do not change after an acid challenge are the strongest indicators of prolonged emotional stress. Emotional habits certainly need to be reexamined and modified.

- **Blue to blue.** Blue results that occur before and after the lemon challenge indicate that alkaline reserve is still functional; however, blue-blues have a tendency to be worriers. Worriers have a problem with digestion because it goes on and on even when you haven't eaten anything. However, they may not have indigestion symptoms. Worry overrides the benefits of any good diet. Consequently, the body is headed toward exhaustion. Many vegetarians fall into the blue-blue category. Because they already eat a lot of fruits and vegetables, they don't need to eat any more. In fact, they need to include more rice cereals with their vegetables to help neutralize the effects of anxiety and worry. Adding more acid-producing foods in the diet might improve pH in this case. However, if worry is the main culprit, serotonin levels will also need to be raised.

- **Green to green.** This steady-state green group is also combating emotional override. These are the "strong emotions" people. Not only are they plagued with anxiety, but fear, anger, and rage may be constant companions. The end result is physical or emotional exhaustion. They have exceptionally low serotonin levels and had no response to the jolt of acid from the lemon. Green means they have some—but limited—buffering reserve left. It is important to make substantial changes in the diet to reinforce reserves of the alkaline minerals potassium, sodium, calcium, and magnesium. They should eat less meat and more vegetables and fruit. It is critical to take hold of emotions. Green to green is not a good situation. This group consists of individuals who are physically and emotionally drained. If you are in this group, you should consider seeing a mental health specialist for professional counseling to help you at this point.

- **Yellow to yellow.** Most people who are seriously ill start with a pH of yellow and stay yellow. The body is very acidic, and the mineral buffer reserve is critically low. But not all people who are in this group feel ill at this moment. This group commonly feels "uptight," requiring tranquilizers to relax, sleeping pills to sleep, and coffee in the morning to get going. Their bodies never rest, even during sleep. Neurotransmitter levels of serotonin, dopamine, and norepinephrine are often depleted or severely imbalanced. The important thing is that, regardless of their present state of health, diet and level of emotional support need to be restructured immediately. Vegetables need to be added to the daily diet. Nutritional or supplemental ways to increase neurotransmitters are recommended. We would encourage this group to seek help with how they are managing emotionally.

Main Points in Chapter 11

- Metabolism depends on how much muscle you have.
- The main ways to improve metabolism include increasing the amount of muscle you have with exercises and increasing your ability to remove acid wastes from cells.

12

Increasing Neurotransmitters and Metabolism Through Exercise and Activity

How many times have you heard that losing weight is simply a matter of eating less and exercising more? While it's true that eating fewer calories leads to weight loss, managing insulin resistance adds another dimension to losing weight. Insulin resistance seems to double the fattening effects of eating carbohydrates—especially around the waist. For this reason we say that all calories are not created equal because they behave differently hormonally.

Exercising Smarter, Not Harder

Just like calories, studies now recognize that all exercises are not created equal. Research shows that certain types of exercises actually end up slowing down your metabolism and increasing your weight gain. I can't think of anything more frustrating than spending countless hours of hard work and sweating without losing a pound of fat. Worse yet, you may even end up getting fatter. Most people think that any kind of exercise produces weight loss. They do not realize that different types of exercises have different results. For instance, cardiovascular exercises improve your heart and lung functions, but excessive amounts actually burn up muscles, upset the stress hormones, and deplete neurotransmitters. As a result, your metabolism slows down, causing you to retain fat rather than lose it.

Excessive exercise eventually lowers the neurotransmitters that support your mood and energy. Jogging was the big exercise trend back in the 1970s. Everybody was hoping to get a "natural high." The truth is, very few people ever produce enough endorphins to feel that great. Overexercising depletes serotonin, which can result in exercise addiction.

"Losing fat" is different from "losing weight." Most people jump on a bathroom scale while dieting and exercising, hoping to see the numbers drop. What they don't realize is that the weight they may be losing could be from losing muscles. Exercising too hard for too long leads to muscle wasting. Having less muscle leads to a slower metabolism and slower fat loss.

Avoiding Exercise Abuse

Your body has a preference as to the exact kinds of calories it prefers to burn during exercise. Whether you burn off carbohydrates, proteins, or fat depends on how intense your activities are. High-intensity exercises such as aerobics, running, jogging, kickboxing, Tae Bo, and bicycle spinning raise your heart rate into a cardio-conditioning zone. These exercises improve the functions of the heart muscle and lungs. Low-intensity activities such as gardening, walking, and golfing increase your heart rate only moderately. Low-intensity exercises are not useful for cardio-conditioning but are extremely valuable for fat burning.

The types of calories you burn during high-intensity exercising can be compared to our example of cooking a steak on the barbecue grill. Consider this scenario: if you marinate a steak (made of protein and fat) in a sauce containing whiskey (alcohol) and molasses (sugar, glucose, or carbohydrate) and then grill it on high heat, what do you think burns off first?

Did you correctly guess that the alcohol from the whiskey marinade burns off first? Recall the spectacle a waiter causes at the table when serving steak flambé or baked Alaska. As you continue to grill your marinated steak on a high flame, the molasses (or sugar or carbohydrate) is the next to burn. Now guess what burns after the alcohol and sugar.

Most people think that the fat burns next. But really, the meat (muscle) burns before the fat. The point is that under high-heat conditions, the fat is the last to burn off.

As with all mammals, cows and humans exhibit similar muscle properites. Barbecuing the steak can be likened to a similar human situation that occurs when you do high-intensity exercising. These activities are rigorous and markedly increase body heat. Similar to the high-heat setting on the barbecue, you first burn off alcohol and carbohydrate calories, followed by burning muscle. With less muscle, your metabolism slows down. Fat is the last to burn when your exercise flame is too hot. Most people don't realize this and work out too hard at body temperatures that are way too hot to burn fat. New metabolic measurement technology confirms this. Recent studies clarify the mechanisms of how our bodies build muscle and lose fat during exercise.

High-intensity exercising requires a lot of glucose for energy. Your body first uses up any immediate sources of glucose. These come from the carbohydrates you ate within the previous half hour. Your next source of energy comes from converting stored glucose, called glycogen, into active sugar. The body stores only enough glycogen for about twenty minutes of intense muscle movement. Once you use up your glycogen, your body seeks energy from the next-fastest energy source, muscle. Getting glucose out of fat stores takes much longer. Continuing to do high-intensity exercising past forty minutes without replenishing your glucose results in breakdown of your muscle. Consequently, with less muscle, your metabolism will suffer. While moderate- to high-intensity aerobic exercises may benefit your heart and lungs, they are not effective for fat burning. Fat cannot convert into glucose fast enough to keep up with the high energy needs required by these types of exercises.

"Cardio" exercises are intended to improve and strengthen the heart muscle. Cardio conditioning increases the amount of oxygen that can be pumped to the rest of the body. Metabolic measurement testing shows that faster heart rates achieved during cardio training do not increase fat burning. In fact, the higher your heart rate, the slower is your fat burning.

Subjects were studied while exercising at high-intensity heart rates until they were "metabolically exhausted." At this fatigue threshold their muscles stopped using oxygen (aerobic) and shifted into anaerobic calorie burning. During high-intensity exercising, energy first comes from using carbohydrates and exhausting glycogen stores. Prolonged high-intensity exercise is hormonally stressful to the body, provoking the adrenals and insulin into "emergency" energy modes.

Even with the results of these types of studies now available, it is still commonplace to see people spending hours doing high-intensity exercises in attempts to lose weight. Uninformed exercise trainers are still convincing people that more exercise and harder exercise are key to losing fat. Exercise physiologists consider high-intensity exercises to be metabolically stressful. They raise core body temperature, dehydrate, and raise stress hormones, such as cortisol and insulin, which increase fat storing. Prolonged high levels of cortisol lead to muscle wasting, high blood pressure, bone thinning, and suppression of the immune system. Chronically stressed individuals who do exhaustive exercising on a daily basis have even been shown to be more susceptible to infections, especially upper-respiratory ones. Overexercising also depletes valuable neurotransmitters. This negatively affects your mood, increases anxiety, increases compulsive thinking and behavior, increases your appetite and cravings for carbohydrates, and interferes with proper sleep.

Exercises for Fat Burning

As a patient cook knows, slowly baking a roast on low heat preserves and tenderizes the meat while burning off excess fat. Similarly, doing low-intensity (low-heat) exercises results in the greatest fat loss while preserving valuable muscle mass.

Metabolic activity testing reveals that fat burns only when oxygen is present. The more oxygen you breathe in and use, the more fat you burn. By monitoring oxygen consumption during exercising, exact "fat-burning" heart rate zones can be precisely determined.

The results of these fat-burning studies confirm that by far the most effective types of exercise for fat burning are those that are low intensity. This is why walking has been promoted as the best way to lose fat. At this level of activity, you can sustain the optimal heart rate for fat burning while causing the least amount of metabolic, hormonal, and cardiovascular stress to your body.

Exercises That Increase Metabolism

Muscle building and weight-resistance training increase your metabolism by increasing and sustaining the amount of muscle you have. Muscles contain energy batteries called mitochondria. The more mitochondria a muscle has, the more calories it burns. Muscle building does two things: it increases the number of mitochondria in each muscle fiber, and it increases the total number of muscle fibers.

Studies show that to best increase your muscle mass, you should use heavy enough weights to produce fatigue of each muscle group.

Muscle fatigue occurs when you have worked a muscle to the point where it no longer can contract or "lift." Muscle fatigue should occur by doing twelve repetitions of an exercise within a fifteen- to ninety-second interval.

Muscle building also requires that you continue to supply adequate amounts of protein to your body each day. Muscle fibers can be made only from protein. Carbohydrates are also necessary for muscle building. They supply the immediate energy necessary to add the protein to the muscle fibers.

Be aware that you don't burn fat during muscle building or weight-resistance training. Weight training actually raises your heart rate into the high-intensity exercise zone. Prove this to yourself by taking your pulse right after finishing an interval of weight lifting. Recall that this heart rate is too high to burn fat very efficiently. The metabolism and fat-burning benefits that come from weight training occur as a result of making stronger and more muscles. Of all the body parts, muscles use up the most calories, even while we sleep.

Tracey, a Fitness Trainer's Story . . . Teaching an Old Dog New Tricks

One of our patients, Tracey, tells the following story:

As a fitness trainer I was teaching three aerobic classes a day. I was embarrassed by the extra weight I still carried around my waist and hips since having my son three years ago. I even lifted weights four times a week. Honestly, how much exercise does a person have to do to lose weight? Dr. Hart encouraged me to have my fat-burning zone determined by metabolic-activity testing, the latest technology in exercise physiology and weight loss. The results of the test told me the exact heart rate zone where I burn the most fat. I couldn't believe that I burned most of my fat calories at a heart rate range between 110 and 122 beats per minute. I usually kept my heart rate up around

150 during my exercise routines. This is what the formula on the wall chart tells us to work out at. Even on the treadmill, the calorie counter said I burned the most calories when I worked the hardest. It took a lot of convincing to get me to intentionally exercise at such a slow heart rate. But I made a two-month deal with Dr. Hart and stayed within my "fat-burning zone" as she asked me to do. Sure enough, I lost fifteen pounds in one month. I couldn't believe it. It was just the opposite of what I had learned years ago and had been telling my clients. What I realized I was actually doing was burning off more muscle than I was making. I'm wondering how many other fitness instructors should know this.

Exercising Smarter

The best health and weight-loss exercise regimen includes all three methods: fat burning, cardio conditioning, and muscle building.

Fat-Burning Activity

Low-intensity activity should be done as much as possible for as long as possible. We recommend at least thirty minutes or more each day. If you are not able to get a formal metabolic-activity test, you can closely approximate your "fat-burning zone" by leisurely walking or bicycling. You will know that you have exceeded your fat-burning zone if you find you cannot carry on a complete conversation without sounding winded. Remember that your greatest amount of fat burning occurs when you exchange the greatest amount of oxygen. Another hint that you are exercising out of your fat-burning zone is if you get hungrier after exercising. This means you were exercising in your cardio zone and used up most of your available glucose. When this happens, your brain naturally sends out the hunger message so you will eat to restore critical blood sugar levels. Most of our clients can't believe how low their heart rates have to be in order to burn the greatest amount of fat.

Cardio Conditioning

Exercises aimed at improving your heart muscle and oxygen exchange in the lungs are done to lower the amount of work it takes for your body to perform prolonged tasks. This includes the effort it takes your muscles to hold up and move your body around all day. A conditioned heart can pump more blood to your muscles. This allows you to burn more fat at lower heart rates. An unconditioned heart has to work twice as hard to pump the same amount of blood out to your muscles. Remember, the higher your heart rate climbs and the longer the duration, the more metabolic stress is placed on your body. Hormones and neurotransmitters react to this stress in ways that encourage your body to retain fat rather than burn it.

Metabolism experts advise that it is best to avoid cardio workouts on the same days you do your weight training. Both of these are considered high-intensity-type activities. When the total duration of your high-intensity activities exceeds forty minutes, they become metabolic stressors. You can minimize these negative effects by resupplying your body's glucose energy source. Eating some carbohyrates after forty minutes of high-intensity exercising keeps you from burning up muscle for energy.

A simple yet extremely effective regimen for cardio training uses the slow-fast interval method. Walk slowly and leisurely for a distance of two blocks (two-tenths of a mile) and then run all out, moving as fast as you can for one block (one-tenth of a mile). Then slow down to a walk and cool down for another two blocks. Rev up again for one block. Keep repeating these slow to fast intervals for a total of twenty minutes. Then you're done with your cardio for the day. Remember to eat a serving of carbohydrates for energy before doing high-intesity training. Drink plenty of water to stay hydrated and to avoid the metabolic stress of overheating.

Muscle Building

Muscle-building exercise allows you to burn more fat calories faster, even while sleeping. Having more muscles increases your metabolism, which enables you to lose inches faster, eat more, and maintain your goal weight easier. This is because the more muscle you have, the more calories you use up to maintain it, even at rest.

We recommend three to four twenty- to thirty-minute training sessions a week. If you are working on all of your muscle groups each time, you should leave a twenty-four-hour break between workouts. This allows muscles time to heal, strengthen, and build. Do not let more than seventy-two hours go by without working on your muscles, or else they will start to weaken and atrophy. It is best to do twelve slow repetitions of each exercise, bringing each muscle group to fatigue.

Remember to hydrate well before, during, and after doing your weight training.

The eating plans B and C presented in Chapters 7 and 13 offer higher-protein options that allow for muscle building. The recommended minimum amount of dietary protein needed for women trying to build muscle should be at least 50 to 75 grams a day. Men who are on a muscle-building program should eat at least 75 to 100 grams of protein daily.

Ideally, you should work with a professional trainer to help you learn the basic techniques needed for optimal development of each muscle group. This is a valuable investment so that you get the quickest results and avoid muscle injuries. There are many good home equipment systems and video programs that will also help guide you.

Throw Out Your Bathroom Scale

During the first month of metabolism retraining, fat loss occurs at the same time as muscle building. If you get on your bathroom scale, you will not see much of a change of your overall weight as this shift occurs. Because we are so conditioned to watch these numbers drop as a sign of success, you will feel frustrated when this doesn't happen. We recommend that you *avoid* weighing yourself but rather track your progress by measuring the inches that you lose. Use the following guide to measure every two weeks.

Inch-Tracking Guide

- It is best to measure yourself wearing the same clothes each time.
- Measure yourself at the same time of day.
- Avoid measuring after exercising. Your muscles will be swollen from the increased blood volume.
- Do not pull the tape too tight so that your skin bulges over the tape measure.

Areas to Track

- **Upper arm.** Measure at the natural indentation where your shoulder muscle separates at the upper arm (biceps).
- **Upper torso.** Measure across your upper chest, above your breasts and across your shoulder blades.
- **Rib cage.** Measure around your middle torso where the ribs meet in the front and the bra line crosses in back.
- **Waist.** Place the tape measure one to two inches above your belly button.
- **Abdomen.** Place the tape measure right below your belly button.
- **Hips.** Place your tape measure across the "perky" part of your buttocks.
- **Thighs.** Measure across the upper widest part of your thighs.
- **Lower thighs.** Measure approximately two inches above your knee.

If you are firmly set on "weighing in" on some type of scale, then invest in a body-composition scale. This special type of scale measures the amount of fat you lost compared with the amount of muscle you made. This is far more accurate than just measuring your total body weight on a regular bathroom scale. Body-composition scales can be purchased at most fitness stores and range from as low as fifty dollars to professional scales costing five thousand dollars.

Main Points in Chapter 12

- The type of exercise you do determines how well you will lose fat, gain muscle, or condition your heart.
- Overexercising with cardio can slow down your metabolism.
- Monitor your progress by the inches you lose rather than by the numbers on a scale.

13

The Feel-Good Weight-Loss Program: Putting It All Together

The goal of this chapter is to help you combine the diet, supplements, and exercise plans presented in this book so that you can achieve optimal weight loss while preserving or increasing valuable neurotransmitters that affect your energy, appetite, and overall sense of well-being. It is designed especially to help regulate the two most powerful influencers of these, insulin and serotonin. In addition, this combined method will help you better deal with stress, get a good night's sleep, control your cravings, maintain a good mood, and boost your sex drive. So far we have focused on each vital part separately. Now we will combine all of them into two effective programs, each with several options. You can choose which best fits your lifestyle, goals, and concerns. The most important way to stay successful with any of the plans is to include as many aspects of your program as possible into everyday living.

We realize that, like most people, you have a zillion things to remember and do on any particular day. It may seem difficult to find the time to put all of these into practice. Even if you can improve just one area of your plan at a time, you will soon feel such amazing differences in your mood and energy as to be inspired to try more. Once you are in "full gear," there may be times, as when you are traveling, that you cannot completely follow the whole program. Include as many parts as you can while on the road until you can get back to your usual routine.

Putting It All Together

We have developed two variations for the "diet" part of the program, Plan I and Plan II. The only difference between them is that Plan I combines linking and balancing for insulin control with three between-meal *snacks* specifically timed to boost your serotonin production. Plan II combines linking and balancing for insulin control with *neurotransmitter precursor supplements* throughout the day as needed to further boost serotonin and dopamine production.

Both plans require the nutrient-, neurotransmitter-, and exercise-support programs detailed here. These are designed for the typical twenty-four-hour day that most of our patients follow. The particular hours of the day may differ from your usual work/life schedule. If you work in the evening or at night, you will need to make adjustments to fit your schedule. The details and the particular benefits of each part of the programs are found in previous chapters. Please review those chapters for more information.

To make things more convenient, you can switch between Plan I and Plan II according to how your individual daily schedules and activities change.

Again, please include the following nutrient-, neurotransmitter-, and exercise-support programs with either variation.

Nutrient Support

Whether you choose the Feel-Good Diet Plan I or Plan II, you need to be familiar with the information we presented in Chapters 7, 8, and 9. Remember, Plan I and Plan II are very similar. The difference is that Plan II raises serotonin levels higher by using supplements. You can combine Plans I and II and use serotonin-boosting snacks as well as serotonin supplements. Follow these seven steps for your nutrient-support plan.

1. Drink an eight-ounce serving of Super pH Water *before* each meal. The serving before breakfast is the most important one.
2. Drink six to eight eight-ounce servings of water or any non-caffeinated beverage plus an additional eight ounces for every twenty pounds overweight.
3. Choose either the Feel-Good Diet Plan I or Plan II.
4. Remember to include at least five servings of foods from the insulin-neutral group each day.
5. Include three servings of fruits every day, linking high-insulin-spiking fruits.
6. Make all of your food choices low-fat ones. Choose unsaturated fats as often as possible. Avoid trans fats.
7. Take a daily general multivitamin and mineral supplement.

Neurotransmitter Support

Pay close attention to your need for neurotransmitter support. If you don't have the opportunity to properly time your snacks, then see if you need to add neurotransmitter precursors to your support plan. Follow these four steps for effective neurotransmitter support.

1. Fill in your "Serotonin Restore Score" log every week. (See Table 13.1.)
2. This weekly review will help you recognize when you need to make adjustments in your neurotransmitter-support program.

TABLE 13.1 Serotonin Restore Score©

This weekly record helps you monitor your serotonin levels. Each week review the list of symptoms and rate them as to how much they are affecting you. Total all of your ratings to get your Serotonin Restore Score.

> **Rate the symptom as 4** if it is *always* a problem.
>
> **Rate the symptom as 3** if it is *usually* a problem.
>
> **Rate the symptom as 2** if it is *sometimes* a problem.
>
> **Rate the symptom as 1** if it is *rarely* a problem.
>
> **Rate the symptom as 0** if it is *never* a problem.

If Your *Weekly* Serotonin Restore Score is:

50–76 This score means you have *significantly depleted* neurotransmitter levels.

20–49 This score means you have *low reserves* of the neurotransmitters. Ongoing stress and dieting will further deplete your levels.

0–19 This score means your current neurotransmitter levels are *adequate*.

SYMPTOMS
Depressed mood
Feel anxious, worried, or fearful
PMS moodiness
Irritable, angry
Chronic pain
Achy muscles
Sleeping problems
Have cravings that occur mostly in the afternoons or evenings
Have trouble limiting food portions
Don't feel satisfied after eating
Think a lot about food
Crave chocolate
Crave starchy or sugary foods
Crave nicotine
Crave alcohol
Fatigue
Have problems concentrating
Have problems staying motivated
Muscle weakness
Weekly Score

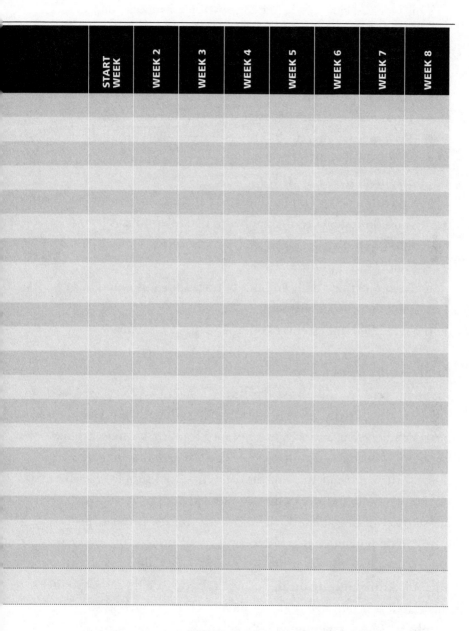

	START WEEK	WEEK 2	WEEK 3	WEEK 4	WEEK 5	WEEK 6	WEEK 7	WEEK 8

Whatever your starting score is, if you are producing enough serotonin from food then your score should be decreasing weekly. If your total score does not improve over time, you need to make more serotonin with Neurotransmitter Precursor Supplements.

This way you can take better control of your mood, energy, appetite, and cravings.

3. Include the following special cofactor vitamins and minerals each day to help your brain produce the necessary amounts of neurotransmitters:
   - Time-release vitamin C ester: 1,000 milligrams daily
   - Time-release vitamin B-50 or B-100 complex: one daily
   - Magnesium: 500 to 1,000 milligrams magnesium aspartate or magnesium orotate daily
   - Calcium: 500 to 1,000 milligrams calcium aspartate or calcium orortate daily. Remember to divide up your calcium into 500 milligram doses to allow absorption.
   - Zinc: 15 milligrams daily
   - Recommended daily amount of trace minerals found in a multivitamin supplement

4. Include 1,000 milligrams of omega-3 fatty acids daily.

Exercise Support

In Chapter 12, we discussed the three different types of exercises: low-intensity activity for fat burning, high-intensity exercise for heart conditioning, and weight-resistance training for muscle building. Aim to increase the amounts of the low-intensity activities you do over the course of the day. Studies show that simply walking a total of ten thousand steps a day significantly improves fat loss. This adds up to walking about three miles a day. Inexpensive step pedometers can be purchased in any sporting goods store or sports department of larger stores. Make an effort to plan for walking and stick to scheduled times during the day or week. Eating a light carbohydrate snack (one serving) before doing intense exercise, such as cardio or weight-resistance training, greatly enhances your performance and results. We recommend doing some low-intensity type of activity every day, with the goal of reaching at least thirty minutes each day. High-intensity cardio exercise should be limited at first to one or two sessions per week. Avoid overexercising by limiting your sessions to twenty to forty minutes. Weight-resistance training is recommended for twenty to thirty minutes two or three times per week. Shorter and more frequent sessions are also encouraged. Consider hiring a professional trainer to help you achieve your goals more safely and quickly. By including all three types of exercises you will be achieving the following:

- Losing fat and not muscle as you follow the eating plan
- Increasing your metabolism by increasing the amount, strength, and tone of your muscles
- Improving your heart as an oxygen-delivery muscle

The Feel-Good Diet Plan I Using *Serotonin-Boosting Snacks*

Plan I combines linking and balancing for insulin control with three between-meal snacks specifically timed to boost your serotonin production. Plan I-A is suitable for most women, Plan I-B for women doing more intensive muscle building and for less-active men, and Plan I-C for men doing intensive muscle building. The specifics of the plans are discussed in Chapter 7.

One serving of a high-insulin-spiking food choice is designated as Hi. Lo indicates one serving of a low-insulin-spiking food. Follow the Hi-Lo patterns of your particular plan. (See Table 13.2.)

The Feel-Good Diet Plan II Using *Neurotransmitter Precursor Supplements*

Plan II combines linking and balancing for insulin control with neurotransmitter precursor supplements to further boost serotonin and dopamine production. If you feel your schedule does not consistently let you fit in enough serotonin-boosting snacks or if your Restore Score

TABLE 13.2 Feel-Good Diet Plan I
with Serotonin-Boosting Snacks

	BREAKFAST	MIDMORNING SEROTONIN-BOOSTING SNACK	LUNCH	AFTERNOON SEROTONIN-BOOSTING SNACK
Plan I-A (weight loss for most women)	Hi – Lo Lo	Hi	Hi – Lo Lo	Hi
Plan I-B (weight loss for very active women and for less-active men)	Hi – Lo Lo	Hi	Hi – Lo × 4	Hi
Plan I-C (weight loss for active men)	Hi Hi – Lo × 4	Hi	Hi – Lo × 4	Hi

Hi = One serving of high-insulin-spiking food   **Lo** = One serving of low-insulin-spiking food

(from Table 13.1) indicates that you need to raise your levels beyond what you can do with the snacks, then follow Plan II by adding the following neurotransmitter supplements to your eating plan. You may also find that alternating between Plans I and II throughout the day works best for your schedule. (See Table 13.3.) As we mentioned in Chapter 7, if you are severely insulin resistant, diabetic or prediabetic, you will be more successful following Plan II.

5-HTP and Tyrosine Amino Acid Supplements

The 5-HTP and tyrosine amino acid precursors to make serotonin and dopamine are available in either oral capsules or in sublingual lozenges. The dose that you need depends on the form that you use. Oral capsules must pass through the digestive system, and so the

DINNER	EVENING SEROTONIN-BOOSTING SNACK	ALSO INCLUDE:
Hi – Lo Lo	Hi	**1.** At least five servings from the insulin-neutral group each day—may eat any time
Hi – Lo × 4	Hi	**2.** *Two to three servings of fruits each day—linking high-insulin-spiking fruits* **3.** The recommended daily amount of serotonin-boosting vitamins and minerals—vitamins B and C, magnesium, calcium, zinc, and trace minerals **4.** Daily omega-3 fatty acids
Hi – Lo × 4	Hi	Avoid eating foods high in protein or mixed with protein in the three hours *before* eating your serotonin-boosting snack. Protein prevents serotonin production, whereas high-carbohydrate (high-insulin-spiking) foods increase serotonin production.

amino acids taken in this way are less efficient. Sublingual lozenges enable the amino acid precursors to quickly pass through your saliva into your bloodstream, and so they are more efficient. (See Table 13.4.)

Doses of Oral Capsules. Start with 100 milligrams of 5-HTP along with 500 milligrams of tyrosine capsules. Take both up to three times daily before each meal. If you still need more help controlling your portion sizes or cravings or feel you need more "willpower," you should gradually increase your dose to 300 milligrams of 5-HTP and 1,000 milligrams of tyrosine up to three times daily.

If the 5-HTP capsules cause stomach upset, nausea, diarrhea, or headaches, you should cut down on your dose. Or, you may find that

TABLE 13.3 Feel-Good Diet Plan II with
Neurotransmitter Precursor Supplements

	BREAKFAST	MORNING SEROTONIN SUPPORT	LUNCH	AFTERNOON SEROTONIN SUPPORT
Plan II-A (weight loss for most women)	Hi Hi – Lo Lo	5-HTP + tyrosine or CraniYums	Hi Hi – Lo Lo	5-HTP + tyrosine or CraniYums
Plan II-B (weight loss for very active women and for less-active men)	Hi Hi – Lo Lo	5-HTP + tyrosine or CraniYums	Hi Hi – Lo × 4	5-HTP + tyrosine or CraniYums
Plan II-C (weight loss for active men)	Hi Hi – Lo × 4	5-HTP + tyrosine or CraniYums	Hi Hi – Lo × 4	5-HTP + tyrosine or CraniYums

Hi = One serving of high-insulin-spiking food   **Lo** = One serving of low-insulin-spiking food

taking a sublingual lozenge form of these supplements may be a better option if you are too sensitive to the oral forms.

Neurotransmitter Supplement Lozenges. As described in Chapter 10, sublingual lozenges offer advantages of bypassing your digestive system. Smaller doses can be used, and so fewer side effects occur. Because the 5-HTP and tyrosine are directly absorbed through the mucous membranes of the mouth, only one-fifth of the amount of active ingredients have to be taken. Our own clinical studies with the

DINNER	EVENING SEROTONIN SUPPORT	ALSO INCLUDE:
Hi Hi – Lo Lo	5-HTP + tyrosine* or CraniYums	**1.** At least five servings from the insulin-neutral group each day—may eat any time
Hi Hi – Lo × 4	5-HTP + tyrosine* or CraniYums	**2.** *Two to three servings of fruits each day—linking high-insulin-spiking fruits* **3.** The recommended daily amount of serotonin-boosting vitamins and minerals—vitamins B and C, magnesium, calcium, zinc, and trace minerals **4.** Daily omega-3 fatty acids *Tyrosine can keep you awake at night if taken in the evening. If so, omit the evening tyrosine dose.
Hi Hi – Lo × 4	5-HTP + tyrosine* or CraniYums	CraniYums Lozenges can be used any time and do not have to be timed around meals.

CraniYums brand have shown that each lozenge acts five times more effectively than capsules. Another advantage of the lozenge form is that timing of meals does not interfere with their effectiveness. Of course, if you are taking them to help you control portion sizes, then you want to dissolve one or two lozenges in your mouth about fifteen to thirty minutes before eating. This way the neurotransmitters will have time to take effect and help you better control your appetite.

With either method, add the necessary cofactor vitamins and minerals to accelerate neurotransmitter production.

TABLE 13.4 Boosting Serotonin and Dopamine with Supplements

AMINO ACID SUPPLEMENT	HOW IT WORKS	WHAT IT DOES	HOW TO TAKE IT	POSSIBLE SIDE EFFECTS
5-HTP 5-Hydroxy-tryptophan	Raises serotonin	Improves mood Lowers anxiety Improves sleep Controls appetite Controls cravings	*Oral form:* 200–300 mg up to three times a day. Oral forms work best when taken before eating. *Sublingual form:* 50–100 mg up to three times a day. Does not have to be timed around meals.	High doses of oral forms can cause nausea, diarrhea, stomach-aches, and headaches *Remedy:* Lower dose or use sublingual forms. Sublingual forms are less likely to cause side effects.
Tyrosine	Raises dopamine and enhances the benefits of serotonin	• Improves energy • Improves mood • Increases metab-olism • Controls appetite and cravings • Improves sex drive	*Oral form:* 500–1,000 mg up to three times daily. *Sublingual form:* 100–200 mg two to three times daily.	Jitteriness or nervousness *Remedy:* Decrease the dosage Can interfere with sleep if taken late in the day *Remedy:* Avoid taking tyrosine late in the day

The following minerals and vitamins are necessary as cofactors for making both serotonin and dopamine. The daily dosages are as follows: calcium 500–1,000 mg, magnesium 500–1,000 mg, zinc 15 mg, trace minerals daily, vitamin B complex B-50 or B-100, vitamin C 500–1,000 mg, omega-3 fatty acids 1,000 mg.

14

Recipes

All recipes include nutrition facts that tell whether they are designated as "Hi" or "Lo" for how much they cause insulin to spike, so you can easily tell how to fit them into your daily meal planning. Some are combinations and are noted as such. Insulin-neutral foods are also noted.

"Hi" means one serving of a high-insulin-spiking food, and "Lo" denotes one serving of a low-insulin-spiking food. Follow the Hi-Lo patterns of your particular plan.

Breakfasts

Breakfast Burritos

These make a great grab-and-go breakfast.

1 medium zucchini, diced
Nonstick cooking spray
2 Boca Breakfast Patties or Morningstar Farms Breakfast Sausage Links
2 omega-3-fortified eggs
¼ cup shredded reduced-fat Mexican cheese
2 whole wheat burrito-size tortilla wraps
Salsa, fat-free sour cream, chopped green onion, as desired

Sauté zucchini for 2 minutes in skillet sprayed with nonstick cooking spray. Microwave breakfast patties or links for 30 seconds to thaw slightly. Chop into bite-sized pieces. Add to skillet with zucchini, and heat on medium heat for 3 minutes. Beat eggs and scramble in pan with zucchini and "sausage." Add cheese, and heat until melted. Divide into two portions. Wrap in tortillas. Top with salsa, sour cream, and green onion as desired.

Makes 2 servings

NUTRITION FACTS PER SERVING (without add-ins): 20 grams carbohydrate, 12 grams fiber, 24 grams protein, 11 grams fat, 219 calories, Hi-Lo-Lo-Lo

Creamy Maple Instant Oatmeal

This is another version of a quick, healthy whole-grain, high-protein breakfast.

1 1-ounce packet plain instant oatmeal or ⅓ cup quick oats
⅔ cup nonfat milk (or ⅓ cup powdered nonfat dry milk with ⅔ cup water)
2 tablespoons sugar-free maple syrup (Brands sweetened with Splenda
        are recommended.)
Dash of cinnamon (optional)
Dash of salt (optional)

Empty the packet of oatmeal into a large microwaveable bowl. Add milk and stir. Microwave uncovered on high for 2 to 3 minutes or until cereal begins to thicken. Carefully remove from oven. Stir in maple syrup and cinnamon and salt as desired.

Makes 1 serving

NUTRITION FACTS PER SERVING: 32 grams carbohydrate, 3 grams fiber, 9 grams protein, 2 grams fat, 169 calories, Hi-Lo

French Toast

Let the bread soak up the egg for extra protein.

2 extra-large omega-3-fortified eggs
2 tablespoons fat-free milk
½ teaspoon vanilla
Dash of salt
2 slices whole wheat bread
¼ teaspoon cinnamon
Nonstick cooking spray or one teaspoon of soft margarine spread (not
    light versions)

Beat together eggs, milk, vanilla, and salt. Soak each piece of bread in egg mixture for 2 to 3 minutes. Sprinkle with cinnamon. Spray nonstick pan and heat, or melt margarine in heated pan. Place soaked bread in heated pan, and pour any remaining egg mixture on top. Brown on each side. Top with healthy soft margarine and sugar-free maple syrup.

Makes 2 servings

NUTRITION FACTS PER SERVING (including margarine): 20 grams carbohydrate, 3 grams fiber, 11 grams protein, 8 grams fat, 152 calories, Hi-Lo

Ham and Cheese Omelet

This is light and fluffy and gourmet—but so easy!

3 omega-3-fortified eggs
1 tablespoon water
½ ounce ham, chopped fine
1 teaspoon vegetable oil
2 tablespoons shredded reduced-fat cheddar cheese
1 tablespoon finely chopped green onion

Using a small whip or a fork, whip eggs and water until frothy. Stir in ham. Heat oil in a nonstick pan. Add egg mixture and immediately shake pan quickly for about 15 seconds. As omelet sets at the edges, lift gently with spatula to allow uncooked egg to flow to the bottom. When omelet is almost completely set, sprinkle cheese and green onion on top. Lift one side of pan, and gently fold omelet in half using spatula or fork to assist. Slide onto plate.

Makes 2 servings

NUTRITION FACTS PER SERVING: 0 grams carbohydrate, 0 grams fiber, 14 grams protein, 11 grams fat, 169 calories, Lo-Lo

Make-Ahead Egg Custard

Make and chill these sweet, creamy breakfast treats now, and you'll be ready for the morning rush later. Cooking them in the micro-wave cuts down baking time.

2 cups nonfat milk
4 extra-large omega-3-fortified eggs
4 packets Splenda
1 teaspoon ground cinnamon
Dash of salt
1 teaspoon vanilla
Dash of ground nutmeg

Heat milk until hot but not boiling (about 4 minutes in micro-wave). Meanwhile, beat all other ingredients together until well blended. Gradually add hot milk to the egg mixture, stirring well. Divide into six custard cups, and place the cups into a glass baking dish. Pour boiling water into baking dish around custard cups until it reaches to within one-half inch of tops of cups.

To bake in microwave, cover baking dish with waxed paper. Cook at medium power (50 percent) for 8 to 13 minutes, rearrang-ing cups every 3 minutes and checking and removing any that are set. Don't overcook. Custard will look soft set. Use a knife to test. If it comes out clean, it is done. Let stand 10 minutes before cooling or serving.

To bake in oven, bake 45 minutes at 350°F.

Makes 3 servings

NUTRITION FACTS PER SERVING: 8 grams carbohydrate, 0 grams fiber, 14 grams protein, 6 grams fat, 170 calories, Lo-Lo

Oat and Wheat Germ Pancakes

Whole-grain pancakes in the morning—delicious! To make ahead, mix up a quadruple batch of the dry ingredients, and then add one egg, a splash of vanilla, ¼ cup milk, and 1½ teaspoons of oil to each cup of mix. Store dry mix in the refrigerator or freezer.

2 cups oat flour
¼ cup wheat germ
1 teaspoon salt
1¼ teaspoons baking soda
1 teaspoon baking powder
2 teaspoons sugar
2 teaspoons cinnamon
½ cup nonfat milk
2 extra-large omega-3-fortified eggs
½ teaspoon vanilla extract
3 teaspoons liquid vegetable oil
Nonstick cooking spray

Stir together all dry ingredients, mixing well with a fork.

Add milk, eggs, vanilla, and oil. Stir with fork until smooth. Pour with ¼ cup measurer onto hot griddle or pan sprayed with nonstick cooking spray. Flip pancakes when bubbles pop, and brown on other side. Serve with sugar-free syrup.

Makes 7 servings (serving size: 2 pancakes)

NUTRITION FACTS PER SERVING: 19 grams carbohydrate, 3 grams fiber, 7 grams protein, 6 grams fat, 159 calories, Hi-Lo

Vanilla Cream Instant Oatmeal

In fewer than five minutes, you've got a high-protein, whole-grain, healthy breakfast—that tastes great too.

1 1-ounce packet plain instant oatmeal or ⅓ cup quick oats
⅔ cup nonfat milk (or ⅓ cup powdered nonfat dry milk with ⅔ cup water)
2 tablespoons vanilla sugar-free coffee syrup
Dash of cinnamon (optional)
Dash of salt (optional)

Empty oatmeal into a large microwaveable bowl. Add milk and stir. Microwave uncovered on high for 2 to 3 minutes or until cereal begins to thicken. Carefully remove from oven. Stir in vanilla syrup and cinnamon and salt as desired.

Makes 1 serving

NUTRITION FACTS PER SERVING: 26 grams carbohydrate, 3 grams fiber, 9 grams protein, 2 grams fat, 151 calories, Hi-Lo

Veggie Omelet

Fit in vegetables wherever you can. Here's one delicious way to
do it.

1 teaspoon vegetable oil
1 cup of any combination of the following vegetables:
    Diced zucchini
    Chopped onion
    Diced red, yellow, or green pepper
    Diced tomato
    Sliced mushrooms
3 omega-3-fortified eggs
1 tablespoon water
½ teaspoon basil
2 tablespoons shredded reduced-fat cheddar cheese or fat-free feta
    cheese
2 tablespoons sliced green onion
Salt and black pepper as desired

Heat oil in a nonstick pan. Stir-fry vegetables until lightly cooked.
Using a small whip or a fork, whip eggs, water, and basil until
frothy. Add egg mixture to vegetables, and immediately shake pan
quickly for about 15 seconds. As omelet sets at the edges, lift gently
with spatula to allow uncooked egg to flow to the bottom. When
omelet is almost completely set, sprinkle cheese and green onion
on top. Season with salt and pepper as desired. Lift one side of pan
and gently fold omelet in half using spatula or fork to assist. Slide
onto plate.

Makes 2 servings

NUTRITION FACTS PER SERVING: 4 grams carbohydrate, 0.5 grams fiber,
14 grams protein, 11 grams fat, 178 calories, Lo-Lo

Lunches and Dinners

Easy Beef and Bean Soup

Use canned beans to make this soup a snap.

½ pound lean (96 percent) ground beef
2 cloves garlic, chopped fine
1 medium onion, chopped
2 teaspoons olive oil
1 15-ounce can white kidney or cannellini beans, drained and rinsed
1 medium carrot, sliced, or 1 cup sliced frozen carrots
1 stalk celery, sliced
16 ounces tomato juice
3 cups beef broth
1 teaspoon finely chopped rosemary
1 tablespoon finely chopped parsley
Black pepper to taste

Brown ground beef with garlic and onion in oil in a large kettle or saucepan. Add beans and all remaining ingredients. Bring to a boil. Reduce heat. Simmer 20 to 30 minutes.

Makes 6 servings

NUTRITION FACTS PER SERVING: 22 grams carbohydrate, 7 grams fiber, 13 grams protein, 3 grams fat, 98 calories, Lo-Lo

Egg Drop Soup

Who knew this was so easy?

2 cups ready-to-serve chicken broth

2 teaspoons soy sauce

½ cup shredded green or napa cabbage

2 teaspoons cornstarch

1 extra-large omega-3-fortified egg

1 tablespoon water

Parsley, celery, watercress, or cilantro leaves or green onions as garnish
(optional)

Heat to a boil 1½ cups bouillon, soy sauce, and cabbage. In a small bowl, stir cornstarch into remaining ½ cup cold bouillon. Add to pot. Heat, stirring occasionally, about 5 minutes until soup thickens slightly.

Beat egg and water in bowl. While rapidly stirring the broth with a fork, gradually add the beaten egg. Continue stirring about 1 minute until egg is white. Garnish with greens as desired.

Makes 3 servings

NUTRITION FACTS PER SERVING: 2 grams carbohydrate, 0 grams fiber, 4 grams protein, 1.5 grams fat, 45 calories, insulin-neutral unlimited

French Onion Soup

There's nothing like a tasty soup to make a meal complete! Studies show that soups fill you up and satisfy your appetite like no other food.

1 medium onion, sliced

1 teaspoon vegetable oil

2 cups hot water

1 tablespoon beef flavor base

½ bay leaf

⅛ teaspoon black pepper

½ teaspoon Worcestershire sauce

2 slices whole wheat bread

2 tablespoons grated Parmesan cheese

Preheat oven to 300°F. Grill onion in oil in a nonstick pan until browned. Add water, beef base, bay leaf, pepper, and Worcestershire sauce. Simmer 20 minutes. Meanwhile, cut bread into 1-inch cubes and toast in oven until dry, crisp, and golden brown. Remove bay leaf from broth. Divide soup into two bowls. Top with bread cubes and Parmesan cheese.

Makes 2 servings

NUTRITION FACTS PER SERVING: 26 grams carbohydrate, 3 grams fiber, 7 grams protein, 7.5 grams fat, 133 calories, Hi

Tomato Bisque

This is a perfect accompaniment for a sandwich—and a great way to fit in your veggies!

1 14.5-ounce can Italian-style diced or crushed tomatoes
1½ cups beef broth
1 cup nonfat milk

Heat tomatoes and beef bouillon to a simmer. Just before serving, add milk, and heat 1 minute more on low heat.

Makes 2 servings

NUTRITION FACTS PER SERVING: 16 grams carbohydrate, 2 grams fiber, 4 grams protein, 0 grams fat, 98 calories, insulin-neutral unlimited

Asian Lettuce Wraps

Wrapping and eating these healthy treats is so fun, you'll want to serve them to your friends.

1 pound extra-lean (93 percent) ground beef or ground turkey breast
¼ cup bottled stir-fry sauce (House of Tsang Classic is recommended.)
16 large leaves of green or red leaf lettuce
2 thumb-size pieces fresh gingerroot, peeled and chopped fine
1 4-ounce can water chestnuts, drained and chopped fine
6 green onions, chopped fine
3 stalks celery, chopped fine
Small bunch of fresh cilantro, chopped fine

Brown ground meat. Add stir-fry sauce, and place meat in bowl. Place lettuce leaves on a serving platter. Place remaining ingredients in individual serving bowls. Instruct each diner to spoon desired vegetables and meat into lettuce leaves, wrap burrito style, and enjoy.

Makes 8 servings

NUTRITION FACTS PER SERVING (using turkey breast): 6 grams carbohydrate, 1 gram fiber, 15 grams protein, 1 gram fat, 91 calories, Lo-Lo

Deli Turkey Wrap

This is a new twist on sandwiches.

1 whole wheat La Tortilla Factory low-carb tortilla
2 tablespoons fat-free cream cheese
2 ounces deli turkey breast
1 lettuce leaf
Fresh basil leaves, thinly sliced tomato, dill weed, sliced green onion
    (optional)

Spread tortilla with cream cheese. Lay turkey and lettuce on top. Top with any optional ingredients. Roll up tightly, and press gently to seal. Roll in plastic wrap for a portable lunch.

Makes 1 serving

NUTRITION FACTS PER SERVING: 14 grams carbohydrate, 9 grams fiber, 21 grams protein, 4 grams fat, 151 calories, Hi-Lo-Lo

Tuna Melt

Tuna is a great source of omega-3 fatty acids. Slim this old favorite
down with low-fat mayonnaise and reduced-fat cheese.

1 6-ounce can tuna packed in water, drained
1 tablespoon Best Foods Reduced Fat mayonnaise
1 tablespoon finely chopped celery
1 tablespoon finely chopped onion or green onion
½ teaspoon Mrs. Dash seasoning
3 slices whole wheat bread
3 ¾-ounce slices reduced-fat (2 percent) cheddar cheese singles

Preheat broiler. Combine tuna with mayonnaise, celery, onion,
and seasoning. Mix well. Spread one-third of mixture on each slice
of bread. Top with cheese slices. Place under broiler until cheese
melts.

Makes 3 servings

NUTRITION FACTS PER SERVING: 22 grams carbohydrate, 3 grams fiber,
18 grams protein, 7 grams fat, 209 calories, Hi-Lo-Lo

Black Bean Salad

Roasted red peppers and cilantro make this salad unique.

2 red bell peppers
1 15-ounce can black beans, drained and rinsed
1 15-ounce can whole-kernel corn, drained
½ cup chopped cilantro
2 cloves garlic, chopped fine
1 tablespoon finely chopped green onion
½ cup salsa
1 tablespoon olive oil
3 tablespoons red wine vinegar

Preheat oven to 350°F. Roast red peppers until skin appears burnt. When cool, peel, remove seeds, and chop. Mix all ingredients in a large bowl. Chill; garnish with a sprig of cilantro.

Makes 4 servings

NUTRITION FACTS PER SERVING: 32 grams carbohydrate, 9 grams fiber, 9 grams protein, 5 grams fat, 202 calories, Hi-Lo

Chinese Cabbage Salad

This is a favorite potluck salad. Everyone loves it. Add sliced grilled chicken if desired to make it a meal.

1 medium-size head of cabbage or napa cabbage, sliced thin

2 green onions, chopped

2 tablespoons toasted sesame seeds

2 tablespoons sliced almonds

¼ cup vegetable oil

2 tablespoons sesame oil

3 tablespoons wine vinegar

1 tablespoon seasoning salt

2 packets artificial sweetener

Combine cabbage with green onion, sesame seeds, and almonds. In a pint jar, mix all remaining ingredients. Add dressing to salad just before serving.

Makes 10 servings

NUTRITION FACTS PER SERVING: 8 grams carbohydrate, 2 grams fiber, 1 gram protein, 9 grams fat, 110 calories, insulin-neutral unlimited

Classic Chicken Salad

Cooked chicken breast on a bed of lettuce—what could be more classic? Try the variations here for variety. Cook up extra chicken on the grill to use later for this salad, or use store-bought ready-to-serve chicken. Choose dressing that uses liquid vegetable oil rather than creamy styles for best health.

2 ounces grilled chicken breast, sliced

2 cups lettuce torn into bite-sized pieces (Choose romaine, red or green leaf lettuce, radicchio, or spring greens for the best nutrition.)

½ cup of any combination of the following vegetables: diced tomato, sliced red or green cabbage, sliced cucumbers, chopped bell pepper, sliced green onion

3 tablespoons your choice salad dressing

Toss all ingredients together with salad dressing.

Makes 1 serving

NUTRITION FACTS PER SERVING: 7 grams carbohydrate, 4 grams fiber, 13 grams protein, 1 gram fat, 96 calories, Lo-Lo

Chicken Salad Variations

Chicken Caesar Salad: Toss with fat-free croutons. Use 3 tablespoons olive oil–based Caesar dressing. Sprinkle with 2 tablespoons Parmesan cheese.

Orchard Chicken Salad: Add a small chopped apple dipped in lemon juice, ½ cup seedless grapes, or 2 tablespoons dried cranberries. Top with 2 tablespoons raw, unsalted nuts or sunflower seeds. Toss with 2 tablespoons of any low-fat vinaigrette dressing.

Asian Chicken Salad: Add 2 tablespoons slivered almonds. Toss with Bernstein's Oriental Dressing or Newman's Own Low-Fat Sesame Ginger Dressing.

Greek Salad

Oopah! This classic Greek favorite adds variety to your salad choices. And it is so easy to make.

3 ripe medium tomatoes, cut into wedges
1 medium onion, cut into wedges
1 large cucumber, cut into wedges
2 green peppers, cut into wedges
1 cup black olives
6 ounces fat-free feta cheese
2 tablespoons olive oil
¼ cup wine vinegar
1 tablespoon fresh oregano
¼ teaspoon salt
¼ teaspoon pepper

Combine tomato, onion, cucumber, and pepper. Toss together all remaining ingredients. Chill well before serving.

Makes 6 servings

NUTRITION FACTS PER SERVING: 13 grams carbohydrate, 1 gram fiber, 8 grams protein, 9 grams fat, 145 calories, Lo

Taco Salad

This Mexican favorite is high in nutrition. It's a great way to throw in beans for fiber and tomatoes for lycopene.

1 teaspoon vegetable oil
½ pound lean (96 percent) ground beef or ground turkey breast
¼ cup chopped onion
2 cloves garlic, chopped fine
½ teaspoon beef broth base
½ cup water
1 teaspoon chili powder
¼ teaspoon paprika
4 tablespoons ketchup
½ cup salsa
1 15-ounce can whole-kernel corn, drained
1 15-ounce can kidney beans, drained and rinsed
10 cups torn lettuce
4 medium tomatoes, diced
1¼ cups fat-free sour cream
1¼ cups salsa
Chopped green onions or sliced olives (optional)

In a large skillet, heat oil. Brown ground meat, onion, and garlic. Add beef base, water, chili powder, paprika, ketchup, and salsa. Mix well. Simmer for 3 minutes. Add corn and kidney beans, and simmer for 2 additional minutes. Serve over lettuce and tomatoes, and top with sour cream and salsa. Garnish with green onions or olives if desired.

Makes 5 servings

NUTRITION FACTS PER SERVING: 52 grams carbohydrate, 8 grams fiber, 20 grams protein, 3 grams fat, 322 calories, Hi-Lo-Lo

Asian Shrimp and Vegetables

Thinly sliced beef, pork, or chicken breast can be used instead of shrimp. For a fun dining experience, use an electric wok and let each person choose his or her ingredients and cook at the table.

3 cups chicken broth

¼ cup soy sauce

Any combination of 3 cups of the following vegetables: carrots, cut at a
　　　slant, ¼ inch thick; broccoli florets; peapods; mushrooms, sliced
　　　¼ inch thick; spinach

1 pound fresh or frozen shrimp, thawed if frozen

Japanese Dipping Sauce (see Index)

Heat bouillon and soy sauce to a boil. Add carrots and broccoli, and cook for 5 minutes. (Do this step on the stove, then transfer to wok if cooking at the table.) Add remaining vegetables and shrimp, and cook 2 to 3 minutes, until shrimp turns pale pink. Remove from broth with a slotted spoon. Serve with Japanese Dipping Sauce. Serve remaining broth as a soup.

Makes 6 servings

NUTRITION FACTS PER SERVING (using a combination of all four vegetables): 6 grams carbohydrate, 1.5 grams fiber, 19 grams protein, 3 grams fat, 115 calories, Lo-Lo

Chicken or Beef Fajitas

You can use leftover steak or cooked chicken breast strips in this quick dinner that is sure to please.

1 teaspoon vegetable oil
1 medium onion, sliced
2 red, yellow, or green peppers, cut into thin strips
½ pound thinly sliced broiled beef or cooked chicken breast strips
    (Raw beef strips or chicken breast tenders can also be used
    and quickly stir-fried before adding veggies.)
2 cloves garlic, chopped fine
¼ cup ketchup
1 teaspoon liquid smoke flavoring
½ teaspoon chili powder
2 medium fresh tomatoes, diced
Fresh cilantro (optional)
4 La Tortilla Factory low-carb whole wheat tortillas
Fat-free sour cream, salsa (optional)

Heat vegetable oil in a large skillet. Add onion and stir-fry on medium-high heat for 1 minute. Add peppers, and continue to stir-fry for another minute. Reduce heat to medium. Add chicken or beef and garlic. Heat thoroughly. In a small bowl, mix ketchup, smoke flavoring, and chili powder. Add to skillet, stirring gently to coat all pieces. Just before serving, add tomatoes and cilantro. Serve with warmed tortillas, fat-free sour cream, and salsa, if desired.

Makes 4 servings

NUTRITION FACTS PER SERVING (without optional ingredients):
26 grams carbohydrate, 10.5 grams fiber, 27 grams protein, 5 grams fat, 192 calories, Hi-Lo-Lo

Chicken and Kashi Casserole

Kashi is labeled as a breakfast pilaf and is often found with the hot breakfast cereals in the grocery store. But it is a wonderful whole-grain side dish for any meal. You'll love the chewy texture in this pilaf and the spices that are reminiscent of stuffing.

½ medium onion, diced
¾ cup diced celery
¾ cup sliced mushrooms
1½ teaspoons chicken flavor base
1½ cups hot water
1 6.5-ounce package Kashi
1 teaspoon poultry seasoning
4 chicken breasts, bone in, skin removed
Mrs. Dash seasoning
Salt as desired

Preheat oven to 375°F. To a 3-quart or larger covered casserole or dutch oven, add vegetables, chicken base, and hot water. Mix well. Add Kashi and poultry seasoning and stir. Arrange chicken breasts on top, bone-side down. Sprinkle chicken with Mrs. Dash and salt as desired. Cover, and bake in oven for 1½ hours. Let sit for 10 minutes before serving.

Makes 8 servings

NUTRITION FACTS PER SERVING: 17 grams carbohydrate, 3 grams fiber, 19 grams protein, 3 grams fat, 167 calories, Hi-Lo-Lo

Chicken in Wine

Cooking with wine adds lots of flavor without fat.

4 4-ounce skinless, boneless chicken breast halves, cut in half lengthwise
¼ teaspoon salt
¼ teaspoon pepper
2 teaspoons vegetable oil
1 small onion, sliced
1 cup sliced fresh mushrooms
4 ounces marinated artichoke hearts
2 tablespoons fresh tarragon
1 cup chicken broth
1½ cups white wine
2 tablespoons cornstarch

Season chicken breasts with salt and pepper. Heat oil in a large skillet. Brown seasoned chicken breasts on both sides on medium heat. Add onion and cook 3 minutes, stirring and turning chicken breasts occasionally. Add mushrooms; cover and continue cooking about 15 minutes until chicken is tender. Remove chicken and vegetables to a platter and keep warm in oven set on low. Add artichoke hearts, tarragon, chicken bouillon and 1 cup wine to the same skillet. Bring to a boil. Allow to simmer about 15 minutes. In a small bowl stir cornstarch into remaining ½ cup wine. Stir slowly into hot bouillon/wine mixture. Continue to simmer, stirring until sauce is slightly thickened and turns clear. Pour over chicken and vegetables.

Makes 8 servings

NUTRITION FACTS PER SERVING: 6 grams carbohydrate, 0 grams fiber, 16 grams protein, 5 grams fat, 148 calories, Lo-Lo

Easy Stuffed Peppers

Make these in the oven or the microwave for an easy meal.

2 green peppers, halved lengthwise with stems and seeds removed
½ pound extra-lean (93 percent) ground beef or ground turkey breast
½ cup chopped onion
¼ teaspoon Worcestershire sauce
¼ teaspoon salt
1 4-ounce can tomato sauce
⅓ cup instant brown rice
⅓ cup water
½ cup shredded reduced-fat cheddar cheese

Microwave Instructions. Place green pepper cut-side down in a microwave-safe dish. Cover with waxed paper. Cook on high for 5 minutes. Drain.

In a separate dish, mix ground meat, onion, Worcestershire sauce, salt, half of tomato sauce, rice, and water. Cook on high for 9 minutes.

Turn peppers cut-side up. Fill with meat mixture, and top with remaining tomato sauce. Sprinkle with cheese. Cook on high for 8 minutes, turning halfway through cooking.

Oven Instructions. Preheat oven to 350°F. Steam green peppers for 5 minutes. On stovetop, brown ground meat and onion. Add Worcestershire sauce, salt, half of tomato sauce, rice, and water. Spoon meat mixture into green peppers. Place in an oven-safe baking dish. Spoon remaining tomato sauce over top. Cover. Bake for 40 minutes. Sprinkle with cheese. Bake 10 minutes longer.

Makes 4 servings

NUTRITION FACTS PER SERVING (using turkey breast): 18 grams carbohydrate, 1 gram fiber, 20 grams protein, 4 grams fat, 157 calories, Hi-Lo-Lo

Ginger Beef

This is a great way to use leftover steak or London broil. You'll never know it's leftovers.

1 pound boneless beef sirloin or round steak

2 tablespoons cornstarch, divided

2 tablespoons soy sauce, divided

2 cloves garlic, slivered

1 thumb-sized piece of fresh gingerroot, peeled, sliced thin, and slivered

2 tablespoons sherry

2 tablespoons vegetable oil

1½ pounds of any combination of the following vegetables:

    Green beans, fresh or frozen, cut into 3-inch lengths

    Asparagus spears, cut into 3-inch lengths

    Green pepper, sliced into strips

Sliced green onion, to garnish

Slice beef across the grain into strips about ⅛ inch thick. In a large bowl, mix together half of the cornstarch and half of the soy sauce. Add beef, garlic, and gingerroot, and mix well. Let stand for 15 minutes. Meanwhile, in a separate bowl, blend remaining cornstarch and soy sauce with sherry, and set aside. Heat oil in a large frying pan or wok. Stir-fry meat until well browned, about 3 minutes. Add vegetables, and continue to stir-fry 2 minutes longer. Add cornstarch mixture. Cook 1 minute longer until sauce is clear. Garnish with green onion.

Makes 7 servings

NUTRITION FACTS PER SERVING: 9 grams carbohydrate, 2 grams fiber, 19 grams protein, 2 grams fat, 123 calories, Lo-Lo

Grilled Pork Loin Steaks with Rosemary

Be sure not to overcook pork steaks. Use a meat thermometer to be sure that they stay moist and juicy.

1 pound thick-cut pork loin steaks

1 tablespoon olive oil

2 tablespoons rice wine vinegar

½ teaspoon liquid smoke flavoring (optional)

1 tablespoon lemon juice

1 tablespoon soy sauce

2 teaspoons Worcestershire sauce

3 cloves garlic, crushed

2 tablespoons finely chopped fresh rosemary

Cut pork into 4 pieces. Place all ingredients in a resealable plastic bag. Shake well. Marinate in the refrigerator for at least 2 hours and up to overnight. Grill or broil pork steaks just until they reach 170°F. Serve immediately.

Makes 4 servings

NUTRITION FACTS PER SERVING: 5 grams carbohydrate, 0 grams fiber, 24 grams protein, 15 grams fat, 248 calories, Lo-Lo-Lo

Grilled Salmon Fillet

Salmon is an excellent source of omega-3 fatty acids. Choose fish several times each week. The fish can also be baked in a foil packet in a 400°F oven for 20 to 30 minutes.

1 2-pound wild salmon fillet
2 tablespoons olive oil
3 cloves garlic, crushed
Juice of one lemon
1 teaspoon Worcestershire sauce
¼ cup soy sauce
Mrs. Dash or lemon pepper seasoning

Preheat barbecue grill. Rinse salmon fillet and pat dry with paper towel. Cut a piece of foil 4 inches longer than the length of the salmon. Brush it with olive oil. Lay fillet, skin-side down, on foil. Curl edges of foil up around salmon to prevent juices from running out, leaving the top uncovered. Spread garlic evenly across salmon. Combine lemon juice, Worcestershire sauce, and soy sauce, and pour over fillet. Sprinkle liberally with seasoning. Place salmon fillet on foil about 6 inches from coals or gas flame. Indirect heat is best. Cover grill. Cook 15 minutes. Do not turn. Check salmon. Salmon is done when flesh has turned paler pink and flakes with a fork. Do not overcook.

Makes 8 servings

NUTRITION FACTS PER SERVING: 0 grams carbohydrate, 0 grams fiber, 14 grams protein, 11 grams fat, 169 calories, Lo-Lo

Grilled Vegetables

Make these on the barbecue or under the broiler. Grilling turns ordinary vegetables into an extraordinary side dish.

1 clove garlic, crushed
2 teaspoons olive oil
1 small fresh zucchini, sliced lengthwise into ½-inch-thick slices
1 green, red, or yellow pepper, cut into 2-inch-wide strips
½ teaspoon chopped basil
Seasoning salt

Mix garlic into oil, and brush onto vegetables. Sprinkle with basil and seasoning salt. Lay vegetables across grill wires. Grill away from flame. Flip to grill other side after 2 to 3 minutes. Serve when vegetables are just barely tender.

Makes 2 servings

NUTRITION FACTS PER SERVING: 10 grams carbohydrate, 0.5 grams fiber, 2 grams protein, 5 grams fat, 83 calories, insulin-neutral unlimited

Japanese Dipping Sauce

Serve with cooked meats, seafood, and vegetables. Or use as a salad dressing.

1 tablespoon rice wine vinegar
⅛ teaspoon dry mustard
1 tablespoon vegetable oil
3 tablespoons fat-free sour cream
1 tablespoon soy sauce
1 tablespoon dry sherry

Blend vinegar, mustard, and oil in blender, or whip with a wire whisk for 1 minute. Stir in remaining ingredients.

Makes 3 servings

NUTRITION FACTS PER SERVING: 5 grams carbohydrate, 0 grams fiber, less than 1 gram protein, 5 grams fat, 64 calories, insulin-neutral unlimited

Sautéed Vegetables

Choose your favorite veggies. Cook them lightly to preserve vitamins and antioxidants.

2 teaspoons vegetable oil
2 cups of any mixture of the following vegetables:
    Fresh or frozen broccoli florets
    Fresh or frozen cauliflower florets
    Onion, cut in wedges
    Carrot, sliced thin
    Celery, sliced into bite-sized pieces
    Fresh or frozen green beans, whole or cut
    Mushrooms, sliced
    Peapods
    Green, red, or yellow pepper, cut in thin strips
    Zucchini, sliced thin
2 tablespoons water
½ teaspoon lemon juice
1 teaspoon soy sauce

Heat oil in a medium frying pan with a lid on over medium heat. Add vegetables. Cook, stirring, for 1 minute. Reduce heat. Add water and cover. Continue cooking for 4 minutes (most of the water will be evaporated). Toss with lemon juice and soy sauce.

Makes 2 servings

NUTRITION FACTS PER SERVING (using a combination of all vegetables): 7 grams carbohydrate, 2 grams fiber, 2 grams protein, 5 grams fat, 74 calories, insulin-neutral unlimited

Southwest London Broil

Slice London broil very thin. This recipe has a mild southwest flavor. If you want it spicy, add Tabasco to the marinade.

1 2-pound London broil (Sirloin steaks will also work well.)
½ cup red cooking wine
½ cup salsa
2 tablespoons finely chopped cilantro
4 teaspoons soy sauce
1 teaspoon salt
1 teaspoon pepper
4 cloves garlic, crushed
1 teaspoon liquid smoke flavoring (optional)

Put all ingredients in a resealable plastic bag, and shake well. Marinate London broil for 6 hours in the refrigerator. Broil 6 inches from cooking element until it is medium rare, turning and basting once with marinade.

Makes 24 servings

NUTRITION FACTS PER SERVING: 0 grams carbohydrate, 0 grams fiber, 14 grams protein, 4 grams fat, 109 calories, Lo-Lo

Fried Potatoes

Cook potatoes in the microwave first, then quickly brown in a very small amount of oil for fried potatoes without all the fat.

2 small white or red potatoes, scrubbed
2 teaspoons vegetable oil
Garlic powder, to taste
Onion powder, to taste
Salt and pepper, to taste

Prick skin of potatoes with fork. Cook in microwave on high for 6 to 7 minutes. Potatoes will be firm. Cut into wedges or slices. Heat oil in a large skillet. Brown potatoes quickly, seasoning with garlic powder, onion powder, salt, and pepper.

Makes 2 servings

NUTRITION FACTS PER SERVING: 20 grams carbohydrate, 0 grams fiber, 2 grams protein, 5 grams fat, 128 calories, Hi

Garlic Mashed Potatoes

For maximum nutrition, not to mention ease of preparation, don't peel the potatoes.

3 small red or white potatoes, scrubbed and cut in 1-inch cubes
Water to cover
3 cloves garlic, unpeeled
1 tablespoon healthy soft margarine
¼ cup nonfat milk
2 tablespoons fat-free sour cream
1 tablespoon chopped parsley
Salt and pepper, to taste

Place potatoes in pot with water, and boil for 20 minutes. Drain. Microwave garlic on high for 30 seconds. Then press cloves with the flat side of a knife to remove skin. Mash garlic with a fork. Put potatoes, garlic, margarine, milk, sour cream, and parsley in a large bowl. Mash and mix ingredients gently. Season as desired.

Makes 3 servings

NUTRITION FACTS PER SERVING: 15 grams carbohydrate, 2 grams fiber, 3 grams protein, 5 grams fat, 153 calories, Hi

Quick Brown Rice Pilaf

This goes from the pantry to the table in less than ten minutes.

1¾ cups chicken broth
4 teaspoons soft healthy margarine
2 teaspoons Mrs. Dash seasoning
2 cups instant brown rice

Heat bouillon to boiling. Add margarine, seasoning, and rice. Return to boil. Reduce heat to simmer, cover, and cook for 5 minutes. Fluff with fork and serve.

Makes 8 servings

NUTRITION FACTS PER SERVING: 17 grams carbohydrate, 1 gram fiber, 2 grams protein, 1 gram fat, 84 calories, Hi

Snacks

Chocolate "Cheer-You-Up" Sauce

Dip fresh strawberries or bananas in this serotonin-enhancing sauce. Or drizzle it over fresh or frozen blueberries or raspberries. Then enjoy!

1 ounce 70 percent (or greater) dark chocolate

Heat on high in the microwave for 1½ minutes. Stir until smooth. Dip or drizzle and eat immediately. Who wouldn't?

Makes 2 servings

NUTRITION FACTS PER SERVING (of sauce): 9 grams carbohydrate, 1.5 grams fiber, 2 grams protein, 12 grams fat, 157 calories, Hi

French Bread with Dipping Oil

Lose yourself in fantasy! Envision that you are dining in an elegant Italian restaurant as you enjoy this serotonin-enhancing snack. Try other flavors of dipping oil. Omit balsamic vinegar and garlic, and add fresh herbs such as rosemary, tarragon, or basil before heating oil.

½ teaspoon extra-virgin olive oil
½ teaspoon soy or canola oil
1 clove garlic, crushed
1 teaspoon balsamic vinegar
1 slice French bread

Blend together oils and garlic, and heat over medium heat until just warm. Pour into center of a small plate. Pour vinegar around the outside. Dip bites of bread into oil, and enjoy.

Makes 1 serving

NUTRITION FACTS PER SERVING: 16 grams carbohydrate, 1 gram fiber, 3 grams protein, 6 grams fat, 122 calories, Hi

Mocha Crisp

Perk up your serotonin and your dopamine with this crunchy treat.

1 ounce 70 percent (or greater) dark chocolate
1 teaspoon instant coffee crystals
1 tablespoon crispy rice cereal

Melt chocolate in the microwave on high for 1 minute. Stir in coffee crystals and rice cereal. Drop onto waxed paper. Cool in refrigerator or freezer, and enjoy.

Makes 1 serving

NUTRITION FACTS PER SERVING: 11 grams carbohydrate, 1.5 grams fiber, 2 grams protein, 12 grams fat, 164 calories, Hi

Raisins Dipped in Chocolate— and Other Things to Dip into Chocolate!

Store-bought chocolate-covered raisins are made with very little real chocolate. Make your own with "the good stuff" to raise your serotonin. Or try covering other types of dried fruit . . . or pretzels . . . or maraschino cherries. What other things can you think of to dip into chocolate?

1 ounce 70 percent (or greater) dark chocolate
3 tablespoons raisins

Heat chocolate on high in the microwave for 1½ minutes. Stir until smooth. Stir in raisins. With a fork, remove chocolate-covered raisins and spread onto waxed paper. Cool in refrigerator, or use the freezer if you need your serotonin boost in a hurry.

Makes 2 servings

NUTRITION FACTS PER SERVING: 15 grams carbohydrate, 1 gram fiber, 1 gram protein, 6 grams fat, 120 calories, Hi

S'more Serotonin Snack

Make these campfire treats in your oven or microwave. I'm not sure which will raise your serotonin more—the chocolate or the campfire memories.

1 graham cracker, broken in half
⅓ ounce 70 percent (or greater) dark chocolate
4 mini marshmallows

Microwave Instructions. Place one square of graham cracker on a microwave-safe plate. Put chocolate piece on top. Bake for 10 seconds, and then place marshmallows on top and bake for 8 additional seconds, watching carefully and removing when marshmallows puff. Top with other graham cracker square. Eat immediately. (This part should be easy!)

Oven Instructions. Layer graham cracker square, chocolate piece, and marshmallows on an oven-safe pan. Broil 6 inches from broiler. Watch carefully while baking, and remove from oven when marshmallows puff and are golden brown. Top with other square of graham cracker and enjoy. (Don't get chocolate on your chin.)

Makes 1 serving

NUTRITION FACTS PER SERVING: 18 grams carbohydrate, 1 gram fiber, 2 grams protein, 5 grams fat, 122 calories, Hi

Appendix A

Studies

Introduction

We tested the effectiveness of the sublingual neurotransmitter supplements at our Wellness Workshop clinic. Forty-two clients were followed over five weeks while using CraniYums sublingual lozenges. Participants completed a fifty-one-point questionnaire relating to common signs and symptoms of serotonin and dopamine deficiencies. We were especially interested in symptoms relating to appetite, cravings, snacking, energy, and mood. After four weeks, the average of all participants reported a decline of 76 percent of their initial symptoms. Ninety percent of all participants reported a decline in at least half of their initial symptoms. Twenty-four percent of the participants reported complete relief of all fifty-one possible symptoms of neurotransmitter deficiencies.

In another study, we measured levels of serotonin and dopamine while participants used the CraniYums sublingual lozenges. The levels of both dopamine and serotonin rose significantly (400 percent or more for the serotonin) within one hour of dissolving just one lozenge. The placebo had virtually no effect on serotonin or dopamine.

A third study looking at twenty-three symptoms of neurotransmitter deficiency was conducted over a six-week period. All participants used the sublingual neurotransmitter precursors three times per day. The test was done as a placebo-based double-blind study. For nineteen of the twenty-three symptoms, the group with the active ingredients reported several *times* (i.e., hundreds of percent) more improvement than those in the placebo test group. The symptoms most improved were appetite control, mood, anger, fatigue, muscle pain, and sleep.

These studies show the importance of supplementing amino acid precursors to raise serotonin and dopamine levels. The sublingual delivery system is easier to follow and more efficient with fewer side effects.

Study 1: Clinical Symptom Improvement Study

Forty-two clients were followed over five weeks while using neurotransmitter supplement lozenges. Participants completed a fifty-one-point questionnaire relating to common signs and symptoms of serotonin and dopamine deficiencies. We were especially interested in symptoms relating to their appetite, cravings, snacking, energy, and mood. After four weeks, the average of all participants reported a decline of 76 percent of their initial symptoms. Ninety percent (90%) of all participants reported a decline in at least half of their initial symptoms. Twenty-four percent (24%) of the participants reported complete relief of all fifty-one possible symptoms of neurotransmitter deficiencies. (See Figure A.1.)

FIGURE A.1 Clincial Symptom Improvement Study

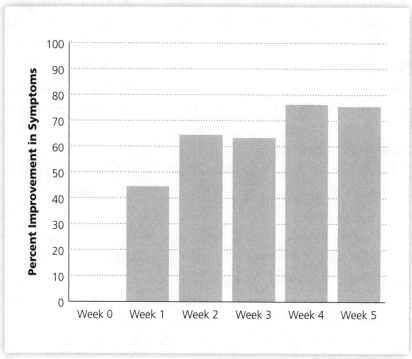

Study 2: Neurotransmitter Precursor Lozenge— Serotonin and Dopamine Study

Participants

Twenty participants were recruited and divided into two groups according to gender—eleven women and nine men. The data subdivides these groups (post-testing) based on whether they received a placebo versus the active ingredients.

Product Ingredients

Proprietary blend of amino acids known to be neurotransmitter precursors were dispersed into a lozenge base. In particular, these ingredients were: glutamine, L-tyrosine, velvet bean extract (Mucuna pruriens), *Griffonia simplicifolia* extract (5-hydroxytryptophan), and pyridoxine (vitamin B_6). These components make up the precursor pathways to both dopamine and serotonin. They are delivered in a flavored dissolving lozenge base of sucralose and isomalt. Commercially, this is available as a product called CraniYums.

Placebo lozenge contained only flavoring, sucralose, and isomalt.

Test Methodology

This was designed to be a double-blind study, with the participants arbitrarily receiving an active ingredients lozenge or a placebo lozenge. Participants were instructed to avoid taking all medications, vitamins, or supplements on the day of the study until they had completed the study. No food was permitted and only water was allowed for consumption until completion of the study.

Each participant provided a predose morning urine collection (second void of the morning). Then subjects orally dissolved their assigned testing lozenge (placebo or active). Participants drank only water and ate no food until they completed their final postdose urine collection between one to two hours after taking their lozenge.

All urine samples were labeled and frozen in the lab-provided vials and submitted for measurement of dopamine and serotonin.

Biochemical Background

The baseline levels of neurotransmitters measured in the initial urine directly reflect reservoir levels of neurotransmitters in the brain. The lower the urinary amount, the more deficient a person is in brain neurotransmitters. With the addition of neurotransmitter enhancing compounds, referred to as *neurotransmitter precursor therapy*, levels of serotonin and dopamine measured in the urine are expected to rise. This rise would indicate increased brain synthesis of the serotonin and dopamine.

Results

The levels of serotonin and dopamine were reported at both the baseline taken before the lozenge and at one to two hours after the lozenge. The summary of the results is as follows (see Figure A.2):

1. **Placebo lozenge groups:** All placebo patients obtained results within a very narrow range, showing very little, if any, increase in either serotonin or dopamine.
2. **Active ingredients lozenge group:** On average showed an 819 percent rise in serotonin and 425 percent rise in dopamine levels. Both serotonin and dopamine increased simultaneously.
3. Although there appears to be some difference based on gender, both men and women had an overwhelming increase in both serotonin and dopamine, as compared to their baseline levels.

FIGURE A.2   Average Change in Serotonin and Dopamine

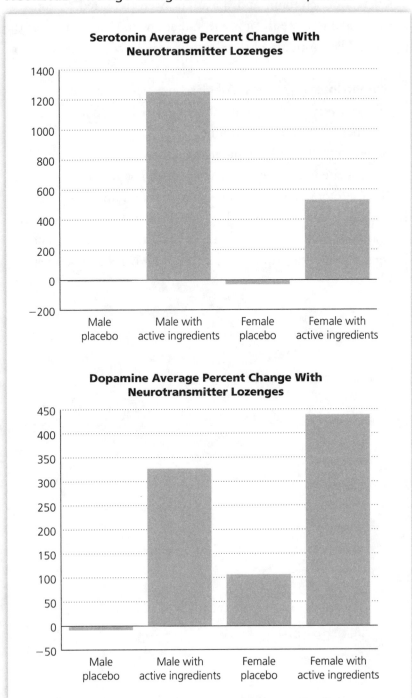

Study 3: The Effect of Neurotransmitter Precursor Lozenges on Symptoms of Neurotransmitter Deficiencies

The study examined the effect of taking neurotransmitter precursor lozenges called CraniYums over a six-week period on twenty-three associated symptoms of neurotransmitter deficiencies. In this double-blind study, sixteen women volunteers were given neurotransmitter precursor lozenges containing either the active ingredients (active) or lozenges made with no active ingredients (placebo). Each group contained eight women at the beginning of the study. One of the "active" women did not complete the study. Each week the participants completed a detailed symptom-rating sheet.

By the end of the six-week study, a significant difference in symptom rating occurred in nineteen of the twenty-three symptoms, when comparing the two groups. The average improvement over all of the symptoms was 3.5 times greater (+350%) in the active than the placebo group. The top seven most affected symptoms were improved fifty-five times more (5,500%) in the active group than in the placebo group.

Purpose of the Study

The study was done to see if taking neurotransmitter precursor lozenges as directed could alleviate the known symptoms of neurotransmitter deficiencies. Since it has been scientifically determined that these lozenges increase serotonin and dopamine—two important neurotransmitters—it was hypothesized that the use of this product would also alleviate the symptoms of deficiencies when the participants increased their internal production of serotonin and dopamine.

Study Methodology

Sixteen women participants who were not patients of Dr. Hart were randomly divided into two equal groups—active and placebo. The active group participants were given the actual neurotransmitter precursor lozenges, while the placebo group was given the same product with no active ingredients. The participants were provided with enough CraniYums to take two lozenges, three times per day—six total per day. They were instructed to dissolve the neurotransmitter precursor lozenges slowly in their mouth and not chew them.

The participants filled out the symptom rating responses on a weekly basis. Each of twenty-three symptoms of neurotransmitter deficiencies was listed in a chart. The participants rated how strongly each symptom applied to them on a 0 (nonexistent) to 5 (strongest) point scale.

Symptoms of Deficiencies

Twenty-three common symptoms of deficiencies of either serotonin or dopamine were on the symptom rating sheet. These were depressed mood, fatigue, low motivation, poor focus, poor muscle strength or feeling weak, anxiety or worry, fearfulness, PMS-related moodiness, irritability, anger, chronic pain, achy muscles, sleep problems, cravings in the afternoon or evening, eating large food portions, feeling not satisfied after eating, thinking about food often, and craving chocolate, caffeine, nicotine, starchy foods, sweets, or alcohol.

Discussion of Study Results

There were originally eight participants in each group of either active ingredients or the placebo lozenges. During the study, one of the "active" participants dropped out. The results from the remaining seven participants in the active group show a decrease in the severity of twenty-two out of the twenty-three symptoms of neurotransmitter deficiencies. However, the decrease in three of the symptoms was not significantly greater than the placebo group. (See Figures A.3a through A.3f.)

There were seven symptoms in which the improvement of the active group was more than ten times ($<1,000\%$) that of the placebo group. These were depressed mood, fatigue, anxiety or worry, achy muscles, sleep problems, and not feeling satisfied after eating (eating satiation).

The active group had significantly more improvement than placebo in the symptoms of fearfulness (500%), PMS moodiness (440%), muscle strength (460%), thinking a lot about food (260%), irritability (210%), focus (190%), craving starchy carbohydrates (190%), cravings in the afternoon or evening (170%), craving sweets (110%), motivation (100%), food portions (100%), and chocolate cravings (50%).

Conclusions

From this study it can be concluded that the use of neurotransmitter precursor lozenges as directed over a six week period affects the symptoms of neurotransmitter deficiencies in the following ways: improves eating satisfaction, improves mood, lowers anger and irritability, lessens fatigue, lowers anxiety and fearfulness, relieves achy muscles, improves sleep, lessens appetite and cravings especially for starchy or sweet carbohydrates, and improves motivation, mental focus, and muscle strength.

FIGURE A.3a Effect on Cravings

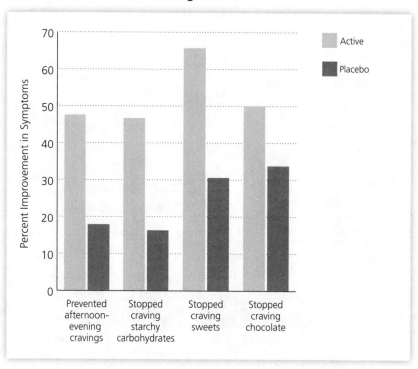

FIGURE A.3b Effect on Food-Related Symptoms

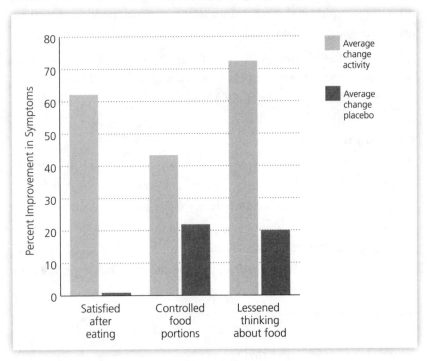

FIGURE A.3c Effect on Mood-Related Symptoms

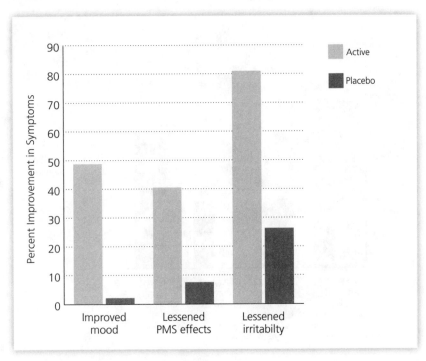

FIGURE A.3d Effect on Sleep and Energy Symptoms

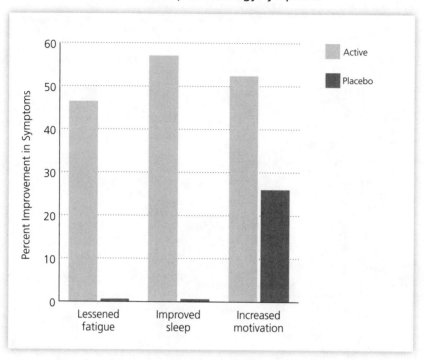

FIGURE A.3e Effect on Emotional Symptoms

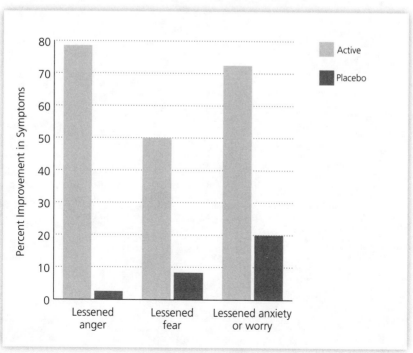

FIGURE A.3f Effects on Muscle Improvement

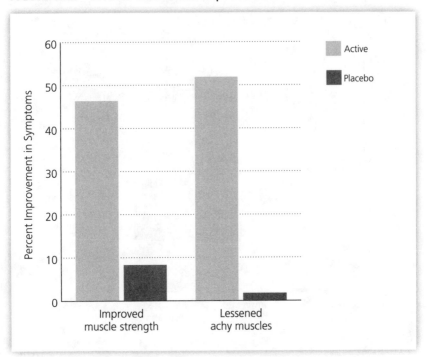

Appendix B

Neurotransmitter Supplement Lozenges—CraniYums

All of the testing cited in this book regarding "neurotransmitter supplement lozenges" was carried out using a product called CraniYums Diet Support. Each lozenge contains 80 milligrams of 5-HTP and 160 milligrams of tyrosine. In addition, another product called CraniYums PM Craving Control was developed with just 40 milligrams of 5-HTP and no tyrosine. This is for the additional serotonin boost that you may need in the afternoon or evening, without any tyrosine.

I have been working with the Crania Company, LLC, to design these products for my patients in my practice at the Wellness Workshop. The first two studies cited in Appendix A to determine how well this product worked were performed at my clinic. The Crania Company itself did the study, a major double-blind, placebo-based trial cited in Appendix A. This was performed without my direct participation, although I designed the protocol for the study.

In Chapter 10, I provided the reader with doses for alternative sources of 5-HTP and tyrosine that can be purchased in capsule form at most health food stores. However, as mentioned, my patients have found advantages to using the lozenges. Until CraniYums are more widely available, you can find out about stores that sell them in your area or purchase them online at craniyums.com.

More detailed information regarding our studies is on the website.

—Cheryle Hart, M.D.

References

Chapter 2

Calder, P. C., and P. Yaqoob. 1999. "Glutamine and the Immune System." *Amino Acids* 17: 227–41.

The Columbia Encyclopedia, 6th ed. 2001–04. New York: Columbia University Press.

Varnier, M., G. P. Leese, J. Thompson, and M. J. Rennie. 1995. "Stimulatory Effect of Glutamine on Glycogen Accumulation in Human Skeletal Muscle." *American Journal of Physiology* 269: E309–15.

Chapter 3

Charles, A. 2005. "Reaching Out Beyond the Synapse: Glial Intercellular Waves Coordinate Metabolism." *Science's STKE* 2005: 6.

Lombard, J., and C. Renna. 2004. *Balance Your Brain, Balance Your Life*. Hoboken, N.J.: John Wiley & Sons, 33.

Meguid, M. 2000. "Disorders Are Caused by Deficiencies and Imbalances in Serotonin and Dopamine." *Nutrition* (October) 16 (10): 843–57.

Melzig, M. F., I. Putscher, P. Henklein, and H. Haber. 2000. "In Vitro Pharmacological Activity of the Tetrahydroisoquinoline Salsolinol Present in Products from *Theobroma Cacao L.*

Like Cocoa and Chocolate." *Journal of Ethnopharmacology* (November) 73 (1–2): 153–59.

Patel, A. B. 2005. "Glutamine." *Proceedings of the National Academy of Sciences of the United States of America* (April 12) 102 (15): 5588–93.

Sakai, T., M. Ideishi, et al. Department of Internal Medicine, School of Medicine, Fukuoka University, Japan. 1998. "Mild Exercise Activates Renal Dopamine System in Mild Hypertensives." *Journal of Human Hypertension* (June) 12 (6): 355–62.

Stahl, S. M. 2003. "Neurotransmission of Cognition." *Journal of Clinical Psychiatry* (March) 64 (3): 230–31.

Szalavitz, M. 2002. "Love is the Drug—Dopamine and Anticipation of Love, Gambling, Eating, or Sex." *New Scientist* (November) 23 (2370): 38.

Chapter 4

Melzig, M. F., et al. "In-Vitro Pharmacological Activity of the Tetrahydroisoquinoline Salsolinol Present in Products from *Theobroma cacao L.* Like Cocoa and Chocolate." *Journal of Ethnopharmacology* (November) 73 (1–2): 153–59.

Volkow, N. D., et al. 2000. "Association Between Age-Related Decline in Brain Dopamine Activity and Impairment in Frontal and Cingulated Metabolism." *American Journal of Psychiatry* (January) 157 (1): 75–80.

Chapter 5

Agid, O., et al. 2001. "Tri-Iodothyronine Augmentation of Selective Serotonin Reuptake Inhibitors in Posttraumatic Stress Disorders." *Journal of Clinical Psychiatry* (March) 62 (3): 169–73.

Appelhop, Bente C., et al. 2005. "Combined Therapy with Levothyroxine and Liothyronine in Two Ratios, Compared with

Levothyroxine Monotherapy in Primary Hypothyroidism: A Double-Blind, Randomized, Controlled Clinical Trial." *Journal of Clinical Endocrinology and Metabolism* 90: 2666–74.

Archer, J. S. M. 1999. "Estrogen and Mood Change via CNS Activity." *Menopausal Medicine* 7 (4): 4–8.

Benwell, M. E. M., and D. J. K. Balfour. 1982. "The Effects of Nicotine Administration on 5-HT Uptake and Biosynthesis in Rat Brain." *European Journal of Pharmacology* 84 (1–2): 71–77.

Birge, S. J. 2000. "HRT and Cognition: What the Evidence Shows." *OBG Management* (October) 12 (10): 40–59.

Bonney, R. C., et al. 1984. "The Interrelationship Between Plasma 5-ene Adrenal Androgens in Normal Women." *Journal of Steroid Biochemistry and Molecular Biology* 20: 1353.

Chen, C. C., and C. R. Parker Jr. 2004. "Adrenal Androgens and the Immune System." *Seminars in Reproductive Medicine* (November) 22 (4): 369–77.

Dharia, S., and C. R. Parker Jr. 2004. "Adrenal Androgens and Aging." *Seminars in Reproductive Medicine* (November) 22 (4): 361–68.

Flood, J. F., and E. Roberts. 1988. "Dehydroepiandrosterone Sulfate Improves Memory in Aging Mice." *Brain Research* (May 10) 448 (1): 178–81.

Foldes, J., P. Lakatos, J. Zsadanyi, and C. Horvath. 1997. "Decreased Serum IGF-I and Dehydroepiandrosterone Sulphate May Be Risk Factors for the Development of Reduced Bone Mass in Postmenopausal Women with Endogenous Subclinical Hyperthyroidism." *European Journal of Endocrinology* (March) 136 (3): 277–81.

Foldes, J., T. Feher, K. G. Feher, E. Kollin, and L. Bodrogi. 1983. "Dehydroepiandrosterone Sulphate (DS), Dehydroepiandrosterone (D) and 'Free' Dehydroepiandrosterone (FD) in the Plasma of Patients with Thyroid Diseases." *Hormone and Metabolic Research* 15: 623.

Hellhammer, J., E. Fries, et al. 2004. "Effects of Soy Lecithin Phosphatidic Acid and Phosphatidylserine Complex (PAS) on the Endocrine and Psychological Responses to Mental Stress." *Stress* (June) 7 (2): 119–26.

Jacobs, D. M., et al. 1998. "Cognitive Function in Non-Demented Older Women Who Took Estrogen After Menopause." *Neurology* 279: 688–95.

Kugaya, A., C. N. Epperson, et al. 2003. "Increase in Prefrontal Cortex Serotonin 2A Receptors Following Estrogen Treatment in Postmenopausal Women." *American Journal of Psychiatry* (August) 160 (8): 1522–24.

Labrie, F., et al. 2005. "Is Dehydroepiandrosterone a Hormone? (review)." *Journal of Endocrinology* (November) 187 (2): 169–96.

Mani, S. K. 2006. "Signaling Mechanisms in Progesterone-Neurotransmitter Interactions." *Neuroscience* 138 (3): 773–81.

Markus, C. R. 1998. "Does Carbohydrate-Rich, Protein-Poor Food Prevent a Deterioration of Mood and Cognitive Performance of Stress-Prone Subjects Which Are Subjected to a Stressful Task?" *Appetite* (August) 31 (1): 49–65.

Markus, R., et al. 2000. "Effects of Food on Cortisol and Mood in Vulnerable Subjects Under Controllable and Uncontrollable Stress." *Physiology and Behavior* (August-September) 70 (3–4): 333–42.

McKuen, B. S., et al. 1999. "Estrogen Action in the Central Nervous System." *Endocrine Reviews* 20: 279–307.

Moses-Kolko, E. L., S. L. Berga, P. J. Greer, G. Smith, C. C. Meltzer, and W. C. Drevets. 2003. "Widespread Increases of Cortical Serotonin 2A (5HT2A) Receptor Availability Following Hormone Replacement Therapy in Euthymic Postmenopausal Women." *Fertility and Sterility* 80: 554–59.

Nagata, C., Y. Nagao, C. Shibuya, Y. Kashiki, and H. Shimizu. 2005. "Fat Intake Is Associated with Serum Estrogen and Androgen Concentrations in Postmenopausal Japanese Women." *Journal of Nutrition* (December) 135 (12): 2862–65.

Pergadia, M., B. Spring, L. M. Konopka, B. Twardowska, P. Shirazi, and J. W. Crayton. 2004. "Double-Blind Trial of the Effects of Tryptophan Depletion on Depression and Cerebral Blood Flow in Smokers." *Addictive Behaviors* (June) 29 (4): 665–71.

Pidoplichko, V., M. DeBias, J. T. Williams, and J. Dani. 1997. "Nicotine Activates and Desensitizes Midbrain Dopamine Neurones." *Nature* 390: 401–4.

Prange, A. J., Jr. 1996. "Novel Uses of Thyroid Hormones in Patients with Affective Disorders." *Thyroid* (October) 6 (5): 537–43.

Rosenbaum, M., et al. 2000. "Effects of Changes in Body Weight on Carbohydrate Metabolism, Ctecholamine Excretion, and Thyroid Function." *American Journal of Clinical Nutrition* (June) 71 (6): 1421–32.

Ross, R. 1984. *Neuroendocrinology and Psychiatric Disorder.* Ed. G. Brown. New York: Raven Press, 95.

Schmidt, P. J., R. C. Daly, M. Bloch, et al. 2005. "Dehydroepiandrosterone Monotherapy in Midlife-Onset Major and Minor Depression." *Archives of General Psychiatry* (February) 62 (2): 154–62.

Shepherd, J. 2001. "Effects of Estrogen on Cognition, Mood, and Degenerative Brain Diseases." *Journal of the American Pharmaceutical Association* 41 (2): 221–28.

Thielen, R. J., E. A. Engleman, Z. A. Rodd, J. M. Murphy, L. Lumeng, T. K. Li, and W. J. McBride. 2004. "Ethanol Drinking and Deprivation Alter Dopaminergic and Serotonergic Function in the Nucleus Accumbens of Alcohol-Preferring Rats." *Journal of Pharmacological Experimental Therapy* (April) 309 (1): 216–25.

Tsigos, C., et al. 2002. "Hypothalamic-Pituitary-Adrenal Axis, Neuroendocrine Factors and Stress." *Journal of Psychosomatic Research* (October) 53 (4): 865–71.

Wolkowitz, O. M., et al. 1997. "Dehydroepiandrosterone (DHEA) Treatment of Depression." *Biological Psychiatry* (February 1) 41 (3): 311–18.

World Book Encyclopedia. Volume 18. 1991. Chicago: World Book, Inc.

Yaffe, K., et al. 1998. "Estrogen Therapy in Postmenopausal Women: Effects on Cognitive Function and Dementia." *Journal of the American Medical Association* 279: 688–95.

Chapter 6

Bantle, J. P., S. K. Raatz, W. Thomas, and A. Georgopoulos. 2000. "Effects of Dietary Fructose on Plasma Lipids in Healthy Subjects." *American Journal of Clinical Nutrition* (November) 72: 1128–34.

Basciano, H., et al. 2005. "Fructose, Insulin Resistance, and Metabolic Dyslipidemia." *Nutritional Metabolism* (February 21) 2 (1): 5.

Bray, G. A., S. J. Nielsen, and B. M. Popkin. 2004. "Consumption of High-Fructose Corn Syrup in Beverages May Play a Role in the Epidemic of Obesity." *American Journal of Clinical Nutrition* (April) 79 (4): 537–43.

Lowell, J. 2004. "The Food Industry and Its Impact upon Increasing Global Obesity: A Case Study." *British Food Journal* (March) 106 (3): 238–48.

Wurtman, R. J., et al. 2003. "Effects of Normal Meals Rich in Carbohydrates or Proteins on Plasma Tryptophan and Tyrosine Ratios." *American Journal of Clinical Nutrition* 77 (1): 128–32.

Chapter 7

Benton, D., et al. 1999. "The Effects of Nutrients on Mood." *Public Health Nutrition* (September) 2 (3A): 403–509.

Breum, L., M. H. Rasmussen, J. Hilsted, and J. D. Fernstrom. 2003. "Twenty-Four-Hour Plasma Tryptophan Concentrations and Ratios Are Below Normal in Obese Subjects and Are Not Normalized by Substantial Weight Reduction." *American Journal of Clinical Nutrition* (May) 77 (5): 1112–18.

Caballero, B., et al. 1988. "Plasma Amino Acids and Insulin Levels in Obesity: Response to Carbohydrate Intake and Tryptophan Supplements." *Metabolism* (July) 37 (7): 672–76.

Fernstrom, J. D. 1994. "Dietary Amino Acids and Brain Function." *Journal of the American Dietetic Association* 94 (1): 71–77.

Fernstrom, M. H., and J. D. Fernstrom. 1995. "Brain Tryptophan Concentrations and Serotonin Synthesis Remain Responsive to Food Consumption After the Ingestion of Sequential Meals." *American Journal of Clinical Nutrition* 61: 312–19.

Ogawa, N., et al. 2000. "Acetic Acid Suppresses the Increase in Disaccharidase Activity that Occurs During Culture of Caco-2 Cells. *Journal of Nutrition* 130: 507–13.

Chapter 8

Brinsma, K., and D. Taren. 2000. "Dieting, Essential Fatty Acid Intake and Depression." *Nutrition Reviews* 58 (4): 98–108.

de Roos, N. M., M. L. Bots, and M. B. Katan. 2001. "Replacement of Dietary Saturated Fatty Acids by Trans Fatty Acids Lowers Serum HDL Cholesterol and Impairs Endothelial Function in Healthy Men and Women." *Arteriosclerosis, Thrombosis, and Vascular Biology* (July) 21 (7): 1233–37.

Food and Nutrition Board, Institute of Medicine. 2002. *Dietary Reference Intakes for Energy, Carbohydrates, Fiber, Fat, Fatty Acids, Cholesterol, Protein, and Amino Acids.* Washington, D.C.: National Academies Press.

Grandgirard, A., et al. 1994. "Incorporation of Trans Long-Chain n-3 Polyunsaturated Fatty Acids in Rat Brain Structures and Retina." *Lipids* (April) 29 (4): 251–58.

Haag, M. 2003. "Essential Fatty Acids and the Brain." *Canadian Journal of Psychiatry* (April) 48 (3): 195–203.

Harris, W. S., Ph.D., and L. J. Appel, M.D., M.P.H. 2002. "New Guidelines Focus on Fish, Fish Oil, Omega-3 Fatty Acids." *American Heart Association Journal Report* (November 18).

Kalmijn, S., E. J. Feskens, L. J. Launer, and D. Kromhout. 1997. "Polyunsaturated Fatty Acids, Antioxidants, and Cognitive Function in Very Old Men." *American Journal of Epidemiology* (January 1) 145 (1): 33–41.

Maes, M., et al. 1996. "Fatty Acid Composition in Major Depression." *Journal of Affective Disorders* (April 26) 38 (1): 35–46.

Nemets, B., Z. Stahl, and R. H. Belmaker. 2002. "Addition of Omega-3 Fatty Acid to Maintenance Medication Treatment for Recurrent Unipolar Depressive Disorder." *American Journal of Psychiatry* (March) 159 (3): 477–79.

Omega-3 oils. 2001. Harvard Mental Health Letter (October).

Salmeron, J., F. B. Hu, J. E. Manson, M. J. Stampfer, G. A. Colditz, E. B. Rimm, and W. C. Willett. 2001. "Dietary Fat Intake and Risk of Type 2 Diabetes in Women." *American Journal of Clinical Nutrition* (June) 73 (6): 1019–26.

Wells, A., et al. 2001. "Omega-3 Fatty Acids in Major Depression." *World Review of Nutrition and Dietetics* 89: 173–85.

Chapter 10

Amer, A., J. Breu, J. McDermott, R. J. Wurtman, and T. J. Maher. 2004. "5-Hydroxy-L-Tryptophan Suppresses Food Intake in Food-Deprived and Stressed Rats." *Pharmacology, Biochemistry and Behavior* (January) 77 (1): 137–43.

Anderson, I. M., et al. 1990. "Dieting Reduces Plasma Tryptophan and Alters Brain 5-HT Function in Women." *Psychological Medicine* (November) 20 (4): 785–91.

Banderet, L. E. 1989. "Treatment with Tyrosine, a Neuro-transmitter Precursor, Reduces Environmental Stress in Humans." *Brain Research Bulletin* (April) 22 (4): 759–62.

Birdsall, T. C. 1998. "5-Hydroxytryptophan: A Clinically Effective Serotonin Precursor." *Alternative Medicine Review* 3: 271–80.

Cangiano, C. 1992. "Eating Behavior and Adherence to Dietary Prescriptions in Obese Adult Subjects Treated with 5-Hydroxytryptophan." *American Journal of Clinical Nutrition* (November) 56 (5): 863–67.

Castano, A., A. Ayala, J. A. Rodriguez-Gomez, C. P. de la Cruz, E. Revilla, J. Cano, and A. Machado. 1995. "Increase in Dopamine Turnover and Tyrosine Hydroxylase Enzyme in Hippocampus of Rats Fed on Low Selenium Diet." *Journal of Neuroscience Research* (December) 42 (5): 684–91.

Castano, A., A. Ayala, J. A. Rodriguez-Gomez, A. J. Herrera, J. Cano, and A. Machado. 1997. "Low Selenium Diet Increases the Dopamine Turnover in Prefrontal Cortex of the Rat." *Neurochemistry International* (June) 30 (6): 549–55.

Ceci, F. 1989. "The Effects of Oral 5-Hydroxytryptophan Administration on Feeding Behavior in Obese Adult Female Subjects." *Journal of Neural Transmission* 76 (2): 109–17.

Heriaef, et al. 1983. "The Treatment of Obesity by Carbohydrate Deprivation Suppresses Plasma Tryptophan and Its Ratio to Other Large Neutral Amino Acids." *Journal of Transmissions* 57: 187–95.

Office of Dietary Supplements, NIH Clinical Center, National Institutes of Health. 1 August 2004. Dietary Supplement Fact Sheet: Selenium. http://ods.od.nih.gov/factsheets/selenium.asp.

Turner, E. H., and A. D. Blackwell. 2005. "5-Hydroxytryptophan plus SSRIs for Interferon-Induced Depression: Synergistic Mechanisms for Normalizing Synaptic Serotonin." *Medical Hypotheses* 65 (1): 138–44.

Turner, E. H. 2006. "Serotonin a la Carte: Supplementation with the Serotonin Precursor 5-Hydroxytryptophan." *Pharmacology and Therapeutics* (March) 109 (3): 325–38.

Chapter 11

Achten, J., and A. E. Jeukendrup. 2004. "Optimizing Fat Oxidation Through Exercise and Diet." *Nutrition* (July-August) 20 (7–8): 716–27.

Fushimi, T., et al. 2001. "Acetic Acid Feeding Enhances Glycogen Repletion in Liver and Skeletal Muscle of Rats." *Journal of Nutrition* (July) 131 (7): 1973–77.

Johnston, C. 2004. "Vinegar Improves Insulin Sensitivity to a High-Carbohydrate Meal in Subjects with Insulin Resistance or Type 2 Diabetes." *Diabetes Care* (January) 27 (1): 281–82.

Kondo, S., et al. 2001. "Antihypertensive Effects of Acetic Acid and Vinegar on Spontaneously Hypertensive Rats." *Bioscience, Biotechnology, and Biochemistry* (December) 65 (12): 2690–94.

McMurray, R. G., and A. C. Hackney. 2005. "Interactions of Metabolic Hormones, Adipose Tissue and Exercise." *Sports Medicine* 35 (5): 393–412.

Ostman, E., Y. Granfeldt, L. Persson, and I. Bjorck. 2005. "Vinegar Supplementation Lowers Glucose and Insulin Responses and Increases Satiety After a Bread Meal in Healthy Subjects." *European Journal of Clinical Nutrition* (June) 29: 2954–3007.

Chapter 12

Achten J., and A. E. Jeukendrup. 2004. "Optimizing Fat Oxidation Through Exercise and Diet." *Nutrition* (July-August) 20 (7–8): 716–27.

Coggan, A. R., et al. 1991. "Carbohydrate Ingestion During Prolonged Exercise: Effects on Metabolism and Performance." *Exercise and Sport Sciences Reviews* 19: 1–40.

Coyle, E. F. 2000. "Physical Activity as a Metabolic Stressor." *American Journal of Clinical Nutrition* (August) 72 (Supplement 2): 512S–20S.

Fernstrom, J. D., and M. H. Fernstrom. 2006. "Exercise, Serum Free Tryptophan, and Central Fatigue." *Journal of Nutrition* (February) 136 (2): 553S–59S.

Fukatsu, A., et al. 1996. "50-Mile Walking Race Suppresses Neutraphil Bactericidal Function by Inducing Increases in Cortisol and Ketone Bodies." *Life Science* 58: 2337–43.

Kajiura, J. S., et al. 1995. "Immune Response to Changes in Training Intensity and Volume in Runners." *Medicine and Science in Sports and Exercise* 27: 1111–17.

Vogel, S. "Vital Circuits" in *World Book Encyclopedia* (2): 424.

Young, D. R., et al. 1967. "Model for Evaluation of Fatty Acid Metabolism in Men During Prolonged Exercise." *Journal of Applied Physiology* 23: 716–25.

Index